PRAISE FOR
FAN THE HOT BLUE FLAMES

Fan the Hot Blue Flames helps leaders, teams and individuals dramatically expand their vision and perspective in solving complex issues, challenges and opportunities facing organizations today. At Rinnai America, the Sales Leadership Team has applied many of the practical, but creative methods outlined in this book to develop breakthrough strategies and initiatives to accelerate our sales growth in the North American Market.

> Tim Wiley, Vice President of Sales
> Rinnai America Corporation

Sometimes you just need a little push to break out of your old habits. Dan's new book helped uncover my biggest barriers to creative thinking. On the solutions side, hours in the day for creative thinking feels like a shrinking ice cube. The idea of combining exercise and with creative thinking is a practical and executable winner.

> Todd Brezler, Vice President of Marketing
> Mitsubishi Power, Inc.

I really love the style and content of *Fan the Hot Blue Flames*! It uses clear language, is actionable, engaging, fun, motivating and right-sized - not too long, nor intimidating. The blend of content, the stories with historical quotes, followed by the fun of seeing it in action in the comic strip stories is great.

The flow is very well done and should work for all levels of experience and knowledge. The comic strip stories demonstrating the tools and value are nicely connected to real life situations and real business problems. I think the balance of substantial content + fun is just right.

Dan Coleman brings the energy – as usual – and makes the knowledge and tools actionable. Now it's up to us – the readers – to apply it and get creative in ways that advance against all of life's challenges!

> James W. Arbogast, Ph.D.
> Hygiene Sciences and Public Health Advancements VP

In his characteristic high energy style, Dan offers a unique approach to developing creative thinking skills. Using specifically crafted superhero characters created to represent the 'Beyonder' abilities of attitude, power and knowledge, he introduces the various concepts that research has shown lead to outstanding results. In addition to simply presenting and discussing each concept, he provides illustrated examples that underscore the key points he is making in an entertaining way. Truly a unique and effective way to learn new approaches and innovative solutions.

> Ray Fisher, District Manager
> Moen, Inc.

Fan the Hot Blue Flames is an action-packed culmination of the best creative thinking and innovation tools available today. The reader will clearly understand the power of creative thinking and how it can increase their ability to overcome challenges and accomplish goals they never thought possible in their professional or personal lives. If you are an emerging leader in a professional organization striving for the benefits of greater levels of innovation for your teams, this book is for you!

Jeff Kesler, Vice President Sales North America
Gerber Plumbing Fixtures

Dan shares his straight-forward actionable techniques to strengthen our **Beyonder Powers**. His creative thinking tools and techniques work in the real world to unlock growth.

Carla Kopyta, Director of Shopper Marketing
P&G

As a leader in new product development for over 40 years, I have been exposed to a multitude of creativity processes. Most are overly cumbersome and difficult to use in a fast-paced world demanding quick solutions. In his thought provoking and clever book, *Fan the Hot Blue Flames,* Dan utilizes a combination of content, real life examples, humor and comic strip characters to tell the story and demonstrate a simple way to teach and use creative process.

Robert L. Quinlan, Retired Director of Engineering
Executive of CPG companies

Dan provides clear, compelling ways to change the way you think about your creative output and your ability to *work out* with passion and purpose. Not only does he provide sound actions to help you reach that highest potential, his focus is tough minded growth with no excuses and an urgency to do it because that is what Dan has done for clients for decades. Dan's solid coaching and training expertise combined with his scholarly credentials in the field of creativity studies takes you not just to the next level but way beyond. You will be introduced to superheros whose powers propel you forward in your quest for exceptional leadership and guided step by step toward your greatness. You will learn what to focus on, what to watch out for and how to keep your momentum going to superior thinking and acting through the combination of creative endeavors and physical fitness, all weaved into superhero stories. As the author states, It's Your Time and your imagination will prevail!

Dr. Susan Keller-Mathers
Associate Professor, International Center for Studies in Creativity
SUNY, Buffalo State

The methods and tools that Dan discusses in the book have proven successful across my Sales, Product Development and Customer Support teams. His unique approach in the book provides an easy roadmap to understanding and cementing the behaviors into habits. With each of my teams, I saw marked improvements which resulted in new clients, reduced contract cycle time, quicker to market product features and better customer satisfaction. Each of my team members learned something new about themselves and was able to demonstrate success in their individual roles.

Louis Rose
Retired Executive, Asurion

Fan the Hot Blue Flames by Dan Coleman is an intriguing and insightful journey that will propel you forward to unlock your creative and innovative potential. I appreciated the novel use of storytelling and superheroes to illustrate how to daily integrate the behaviors necessary to create and master our pursuits. He firmly challenges us to soar, "look past barriers in your life (real or imagined) and reach for that shining star!" I am reminded through his use of best practices, tested concepts, models and tools that we all have music inside and we must "reach way down into our belly, pull it up and belt it out *time after time*." *Fan the Hot Blue Flames* is more than a good read, it introduces a new way of pursuing our most sought-after goals and fundamentally our ever-elusive purpose - CHALLENGE ACCEPTED!!!

Renita L. Jefferson, MBA, GPCC, PCC
Global HR Executive

This book provides an excellent roadmap to jump start your creative thinking individually or as a team and with a fun and memorable approach. I have personally used the concepts and applied the tools that are presented. I have been able to identify problems more effectively, generate more ideas, and in the end implement better solutions through the teachings in these pages. I highly recommend giving your creative juices a chance to exercise and strengthen through exploring this author's book. Dan Coleman is a competent, energetic, and dynamic leader that has conducted training sessions all over the country. I have seen multiple organizations benefit from introducing and implementing many of the concepts and tools he developed. "*Fan the Hot Blue Flames*" and strengthen your creative muscles!

Robb Struckel
Director of National Accounts, Retail, Turf & Irrigation
ADS

FAN THE HOT BLUE FLAMES

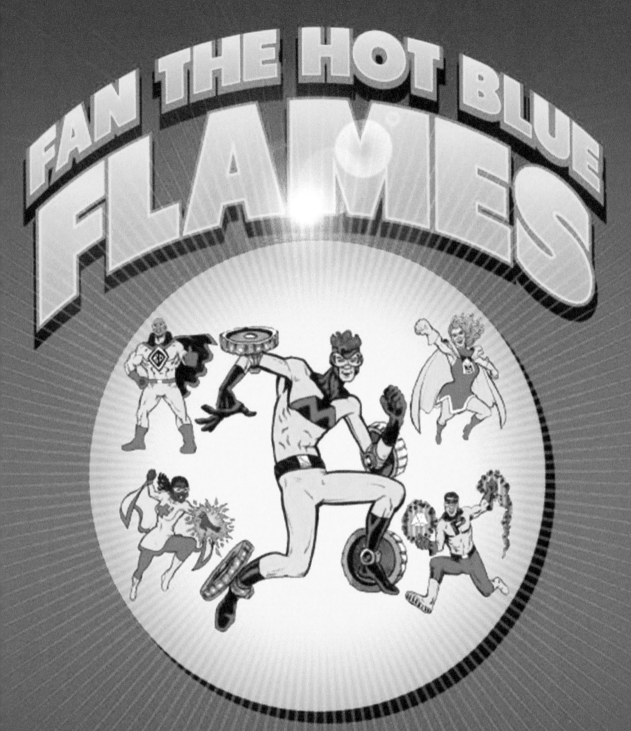

A DYNAMIC METHOD TO **_JUMP SPARK_** YOUR CREATIVITY AND INNOVATION

DAN COLEMAN

Chautauqua Press
Williamsville, NY 14221

Printed in the United States of America

Publisher's Cataloging-in-Publication data
Coleman, Daniel W.

ISBN 978-1-64184-589-2

Illustration by Donald Jackson and Mark Stoddard

Graphic design: Chris Laski and Julie Coleman

Cover design: Lewis Agrell

Print design: JETLAUNCH

Editing: Randy Wood and Katie Coleman

ACKNOWLEDGMENTS

Although I conceived and wrote this book, it really is a reflection of my life and the collaboration, friendship and love from so many people. Yes, it is a combination book, creative thinking program and toolkit packaged together as one. And yes, it represents a culmination of experiences, interactions, collaborations and friendships that have taken place in my life over the past few decades that I must say I am humbled by and profoundly grateful for.

Early on, my mom and dad always had my back, always encouraged me to keep moving forward, to persevere, to get up and brush myself off after a skirmish, setback or disappointment, and most importantly to stay in the fight. Yes, they taught me to go after and stay after the dream. We all have dreams, all different, and we all need to give ourselves a good shot of calcium in the backbone, go and stay after the dream. Sure, along the way there are twists, sharp hairpin and sometimes wrong turns, stops and starts, steep inclines, some black ice and limited visibility because of the thick fog. But so what? Go after it, experiment, learn, adjust and persevere. Moving forward is what this book/program/toolkit is all about!

Along my journey I have been blessed to have worked with and collaborated with so many great clients and trained thousands of wonderful people in my workshops. At the risk of not mentioning someone I should, I'd like to give a special call-out thank you to Phil Burne, Dan Porter, Sean O'Donnell, Renita Jefferson, Carla Kopyta, Brian Grenfell, Ray Fisher, Kris Mason, Tim Wiley, Paige Giannetti, Jim Arbogast, Tim Dye, Argerie Vasilakes, Christine Hoffer, Robb Struckel, Mark Savan, Louis Rose, Bob Quinlan, Chris Banning, Jeff Kesler, Todd Brezler, Steve Beall, Terry Craig, Pat Virost, Ethel Vinson, Steve Smith, Kelly Loebick-Frascella, Tim Shearer, Inge Orendt, Rich Somplatsky, Grant Marquit, Dan Fisher, Moises Solis, Steve Cohen, Gerard Puccio, Mary Murdock, Susan Keller-Mathers, Roger Firestein and Mike Fox. Each one of them, in their own way, helped me to grow.

This book could not have been developed without the tireless and creative efforts of my editors Randy Wood and Katie Coleman; internal book designer Rae Cuddle, graphic designers Chris Laski and Julie Coleman, artist/illustrators Don Jackson and Mark Stoddard and book cover designer Lewis Agrell. I am grateful for their unique insight, talent and collaborative attitude.

Lastly, a special thanks to my beautiful wife Jan and daughters Jill, Katie, Julie and Samantha for their unwavering support, encouragement and love. I am truly blessed.

DEDICATION

I dedicate this book to my Mom and Dad, my wife Jan,
and my daughters Jill, Katie, Julie and Samanatha.

CONTENTS

JUST WARMING UP

PURPOSE

It is with *good energy* that I welcome you! The very fact that you are holding this program in your hands right now is indicative of your willingness to step outside traditional means and methods to consider a new approach. From this first moment of openness you are now demonstrating—to where I believe this journey can take you—is nothing short of remarkable. I know because I've been *sparking* individuals and teams to think and act more creatively for over two decades and the results are among the most enlivening and energetic aspects of business life.

After having success in seminar environments for years, I began to wonder in what ways I might **X**celerate the use of creativity tools and techniques even further into the everyday lives of individuals and teams. This dynamic program is the result of that effort.

Program Alert: This program *is not designed* to be a casual bedtime read, plenty of other options for that. Rather it is designed for people who **dare to accept the challenge** – who very much want to sharpen their creative skills to a razors edge – to get *creativity fit* in order to fully embark on important challenges, solve tough problems and pursue opportunities in a fresh and energetic way. In this program you have access to a bottomless bag of tips, tricks, tools, techniques, Two-Board Adjustments (ways to anchor creative thinking as a habit) and **Workouts** (divergent and convergent creative thinking tools) to guide you through your previously unchartered regions of thinking, perceiving and acting more creatively. I guarantee that what you will discover on this journey will invigorate you as nothing else has. One simple ground rule – you must do the work! This program is 100% based on your effort, applying yourself, reflecting on your results and adapting. If you are willing to do the work, I am very confident you will be quite pleased with your results. The primary objectives of this program are to:

- Train your technique and strengthen your *B e y o n d e r Powers* (creative thinking skills). You will meet and learn more about the five *B e y o n d e r s* (superheroes with creative *Powers*) in the next section.
- Anchor creative thinking and physical exercise (a bonus) as repeatable, everyday habits.

- Increase your innovation productivity (the implementation of novel and feasible ideas/concepts) that were fueled by creative thinking.
- *Lean into Risk, Embrace Your Dream and Take Proactive Actions to go get it!*

How's that for Ennnnnnergy? The good news is you don't have to take more stuff from the outside and shove it in. *Rather, it's to liberate more of the good stuff that's already in you, get it out and get it to action!* Did I mention *action*? You have the natural creative capabilities, the horsepower. The challenge at hand is to use the tips, tricks, tools, techniques, Two-Board Adjustments and **Workouts**, to strengthen and **X**celerate the good stuff to full power and anchor it as a repeatable, everyday habit!

Sure, there are **Resistors** to creativity (forces that inhibit creativity). You will meet and learn more about the five **Resistors** in the next section. They lurk in the shadows, the cowards. The required action is to shine a bright light on them and conquer these villains. After all, life is far too short not to. Yes, it takes attitude, calcium in the backbone, energy, persistence and smarts to *Lean into Risk, Embrace Your Dream and Take Proactive Actions to go get it!* There is nothing more powerful than a compelling *Dream*, even if it may appear to be somewhat out of reach at this moment. And a *Dream* without proactive, focused action is simply a group of nice happy thoughts—which are not the target! The target is to develop and combine your compelling *Dream* with proactive, focused action to *jump spark* your imagination, get traction and propel yourself forward now! You will forge a dogged determination. You will fight and persevere through the bumps, the battles, the doubts and the rough spots. Yes, you will prevail and triumph!

PROCESS AT A GLANCE

In this program you will liberate your *B e y o n d e r Powers*, conquer **The Resistors** to creativity and navigate the whitewater rapids of thinking, perceiving and acting more creatively. Following is the flow of the program:

- In What's Stopping You, you meet *The B e y o n d e r s* and **The Resistors.**

- In each of the three **Episodes** – **Episode i** (Fight the Right Foe); **Episode ii** (Imagination will Prevail); and **Episode iii** (The Power of Speed) you:

  - Establish a cadence and explore the *bursts* of content that describe the restraining forces of the **Resistors** and the liberating *Powers* of the *B e y o n d e r s*.
  - Witness a **Battle** in the comic strip where a *B e y o n d e r* summons their *Powers* to conquer the restraining forces of the **Resistor(s)**.
  - Review a profile of a person that exemplified the content highlighted in the **Episode**.
  - Segue to the It's Your Time section (the idea sparked by Dr. Susan Keller-Mathers and Dr. Mary Murdock (2008) in their application of Step 3 - Extending the Learning from the Torrance Incubation Model) that follows each **Battle** and apply the **Divergent and Convergent Workouts** used in the comic strip to your specific Dream/Big Goal. Note: The source for many of the **Workouts** in these sections is The Center for Applied Imagination at SUNY Buffalo State College. They have been adapted to better align with the *Powers* of the *B e y o n d e r s*.

The Appendix (Get Creativity Fit®) is organized as follows:

  - Appendix A, **Upward**, contains two surveys to assess your frequency in using the fifteen *B e y o n d e r Powers* and to baseline your current creative productivity.
  - Appendix B, **Anchor the Creative and Physical Exercise Habits**, provides a 28 day framework for you to anchor creative thinking and physical exercise as repeatable, everyday habits. There are four weekly planning templates to use. The central idea is to *work out* with **Divergent and Convergent Workouts** every day for 28 straight days and apply them to your Dream/Big Goal. By doing this you will strengthen your skills and be poised to *Lean into Risk, Embrace Your Dream and Take Proactive Actions to go get it.* You will also increase your odds of anchoring creative thinking and physical exercise as a repeatable, everyday habit. **Note:** The physical exercise component is optional, yet highly recommended. It is included as an extra bonus option for people who would like to do it. The primary reasons are that physical

exercise is good for the body; it builds muscle and conditions the heart and the lungs. It also builds, conditions and influences the brain. The brain is an adaptable organ that can be shaped similarly to the way muscles can be strengthened. The more we exercise the stronger and more versatile the brain becomes.

HOW TO SQUEEZE THE MOST JUICE OUT OF THIS PROGRAM?

There are many paths you can take to squeeze the most **fresh-squeezed juice** full of sweet pulp out of this program. You work the program the program doesn't work for you. Following is one of the recommended paths:

- Read the **What's Stopping You Section**.
- Go to Appendix A, take the *B e y o n d e r Powers Survey* and the Creative Productivity Snapshot Survey. Assess your starting point and establish your goals for your creative thinking and physical exercise before you really get going. Review the planning sheets and set your 1st cut goals. Note: The **Dare to Dream Workout** located in **Episode I**, **Battle #1** is designed to help you define and establish your Dream/Big Goal.
- Enough of getting organized. Return to **Episode I**, start the 28 day clock, and *X*celerate your pace with unbridled enthusiasm!

What's Stopping You?

THE RESISTORS VS THE BEYONDERS

THE
BEYONDERS
FACE OFF WITH THE RESISTORS

ONWARD & UPWARD

Every renaissance comes to the world with a cry,
the cry of the human spirit to be free.

— Anne Sullivan Macy, teacher and lifelong companion of Helen Keller

A cornerstone of this program is the belief that we were all born with a resilient creative spirit and an innate ability to think, perceive and act creatively. The natural capacity is in you, always has been and now it's time to rekindle it and *liberate more of the good stuff*. My guess is you don't remember learning how to walk or talk. You used your natural abilities, aided by encouragement from loved ones to accomplish these tasks. Unfortunately, we've gotten away from consistently using our natural creative capacity. No more — we're going to develop our ability to make the skills available on demand, any time, any place.

The B e y o n d e r s and **The Resistors** were created to help *jump spark* your creative *Powers*. I must confess, there is not an exact, early-detection system that will predict which **Resistors** will appear whenever and wherever you may be in your creative effort. They don't care; they just want to derail you. They may come at you solo or in tandem, but at least one of them is always there in the shadows where you can't see them (the cowards). Given this, the proactive action to conquer them is to have a good offense. Take it from a former field lacrosse defenseman: the best defense is a really good offense with the ball at the other end of the field in the attack zone where it belongs, away from my goal. And speaking of a really good offense....

THE BEYONDER CONCEPT

Paul Torrance (1999) was a pioneering creativity researcher and developed a rich body of materials to assess and teach creative thinking. He introduced the Beyonder Concept when explaining the achievements of people who were administered the Torrance Test of Creative Thinking thirty years prior, when they were high school students. He reported that a small number of people with many distinct creative achievements were worthy of their own category because they rated well above the other high creative achievers. He reduced the initial 35 characteristics down to the ten that distinguished The Beyonders:

Delight in Deep Thinking	Tolerance of Mistakes
Love of One's Work	Clear Purpose
Enjoying One's Work	Feel Comfortable as a Minority of One
Being Different	Not Being Well-Rounded
Sense of Mission in Life	Courage to be Creative

Torrance's groundbreaking work sparked me to leverage The Beyonder Concept and develop a dynamic method for individuals and teams to be able to summon their skills on the spot, any time, any place. Sounds really cool, don't you think? Let's take an adventurous journey together!

BE A BEYONDER

We're all absolutely equal in having the opportunity to make the most of what we have.

— John Wooden, college basketball coaching legend

Be a Beyonder means to elevate your game in three areas:

- **Attitude**
- **Powers**
- **Knowledge**

ATTITUDE

A *Beyonder* has an attitude about living a creative life. Here we zero in on two *Beyonder* characteristics, with the tagline, "*Can't worry much about what others think.*"

Be bold and break free from the herd. Author and humorist Lewis Grizzard said, "*If you ain't the lead dog the scenery never changes.*" The lead dogs on a sledding team steer the team and set the pace, and clearly have the best, unobstructed view. Social conformity, the fear of not fitting in (remember junior high school?), is one strong **Resistor** that inhibits us from taking risks and *breaking from the herd*.

In his best-selling book Influence, Robert Cialdini (2009) described the principle of *social proof*. If many other people are doing it, it must be right. Translation: *the herd made me do it*! As the story (or fable) goes, Ernest Shackleton (Schultz, 2013) ran a newspaper ad in the early 1900s recruiting men for his endurance expedition to the South Pole:

Men wanted for hazardous journey to the South Pole. Small wages, bitter cold, long months of complete darkness, constant danger. Safe return doubtful. Honor and recognition in case of success.

Yes, this exhibits bold behavior that breaks from the herd. *Embrace experimenting, take risks (many small ones are welcome), quickly learn, adapt and tolerate failure.* Ahh, the dreaded enemy—*failure*! How about we reframe how we think about *failure*? In 1941, Ted Williams hit .406, the last professional baseball player to reach that elusive milestone; no one has hit .400 since. He was a six-time batting champion with a lifetime .344 average. His *failure rate* in 1941 was .594 and .656 over his nineteen-year, hall-of-fame career. Many baseball historians recognize Williams as the best hitter in the history of major league baseball. His career was not a failure, not a *lack of success*—it was just the opposite!

Nothing big happens without an attitude of experimenting. Without it, the training programs, innovation processes, bumper sticker declarations and good-looking PowerPoint presentations fall way short and deliver dismal results. Maintaining the status-quo, playing it safe, being overly risk-averse is simply not an option. In fact, it's annoying, and downright boring! *You're boring me*! Grant yourself the freedom *today* and adopt this attitude to significantly improve your current situation. Your innovation altitude will be determined by the sheer force of your *forward-leaning B e y o n d e r* Attitude! How's that for *energy*?

POWERS

A *B e y o n d e r* has *highly developed divergent and convergent thinking Powers*. In this program the term *Powers* is used interchangeably with skills (it's just more powerful). The creative muscles must be readily available to produce novel and feasible thinking. With our skeletal frame, muscle growth occurs when the rate of muscle protein synthesis is greater than the rate of muscle protein breakdown. You've got to use them and rest in between because that is when muscle growth occurs. The same is true for divergent and convergent thinking. *Divergent thinking* facilitates going beyond current boundaries, drawing out specific meanings and producing an abundance of novel ideas. *Convergent thinking* is necessary to tame the novel thinking, to strengthen and select ideas and options to be feasible. The growth occurs when you transition between alternating divergent and convergent thinking and separate it with some time in between.

Successful sports teams have well-conditioned athletes, specialized coaching, game strategies and a playbook for different game situations. The elite teams have an additional, elusive element that separates them from the pack. They have the players with superior skills to consistently execute the plays, time and again. These athletes continually train and perfect their technique to maintain their skill and fitness edge. Same principle holds true here: you have to train and perfect your divergent and convergent thinking skills. Following are the fifteen *B e y o n d e r Powers* (adapted from Torrance, 1999).

THE B E Y O N D E R POWERS

Find It	Be Fluent	Borrow It	Put Ideas in Context	Be Optimistic
See It	Be Novel	Elaborate	Evaluate and Select It	Use Humor and Intuition
Be Versatile	Stay Open	Make New Combinations	Strengthen It	Act on It

Additive to the *Powers* are personality traits. A host of creativity researchers (Amabile, 1996; Davis, 2004; Sternberg, 1999; and Torrance, 1999) among many others have identified the following personality traits that correlate with increased levels of creative behavior. Not all people possess all the traits (a pretty tall order). And some of the traits conflict with one another.

PERSONALITY TRAITS

Awareness of Creativeness	Original	Independent	Risk Taking
High Energy	Curious	Sense of Humor	Capacity for Fantasy
Attracted to Complexity and Ambiguity	Artistic	Open Minded	Thorough
Needs Alone Time	Perceptive	Emotional	Ethical
Self-Disciplined	Focused	Persevering Work Style	Intrinsic Focus on Excellence

KNOWLEDGE

A *B e y o n d e r* becomes knowledgeable in the areas where they are pursuing their *Dream/Big Goal* and need to produce more innovation. This includes a familiarity with the facts, technical knowledge, information, principles and opinions of subject-matter experts in the targeted area. For example, if you want to generate new ideas in the area of molecular biology it's a prerequisite you have a baseline knowledge of molecular biology— better yet, a keen insight about molecular biology. Yes, it's possible you may get lucky and be struck by a spontaneous idea—the right place at the right time (even a blind squirrel can find a nut from time to time). However, hope is not a good repeatable strategy. You are most likely to gain unique insight and knowledge and generate novel ideas when you are familiar with a subject, immerse yourself and study it intently. Albert Szent-Gyorgyi (Carson, 1965), a Hungarian biochemist who won the Nobel Prize in Physiology or Medicine in 1937, discovered Vitamin C, the components and reactions of the citric acid cycle. He said, "Discovery consists of looking at the same thing as everyone else and thinking something different. A discovery is an accident meeting a prepared mind."

Combining the key ingredients of **Attitude**, *Powers* and **Knowledge** make for a powerful creativity brew to identify and solve the right problems; pursue the best opportunities; generate novel ideas; strengthen and make the best ideas feasible; and catapult them to action… now! Just need to give the brew a real good stirring every day.

A *B e y o n d e r* has a striking resemblance to *Superheroes,* don't you think? In his book, *Superman On The Couch: What Superheroes Really Tell Us about Ourselves and Our Society*, Danny Fingeroth (2004) provides a history of superheroes and why they have captured the imagination of people of all ages, backgrounds and from different generations. He identifies a few key characteristics:

- They have fantastic powers (whether magic or science-based) and battle their antagonists with advanced technology.
- They possess skills and abilities normal humans don't have. For example, on a daily basis Batman leaps unarmed into gunfire and mutant-powered muscle and comes out with nary a scratch.
- They represent the values of the society that produces them. The most obvious things are strength of character, some system of positive values and a determination to protect those values no matter what.
- The hero does the right thing. In fact, they know what the right thing is.
- They have a never-say-die attitude.

A *B e y o n d e r* does possess *Superhero Powers* with three caveats. Like you and me:

- Even though they're blessed with individual *Powers* they gain a good deal of their strength by working together.
- They are fallible and because of this they take steps to compensate for it by leveraging their individual and collective *Powers*.
- They are most formidable when they use available resources and consistently engage in Divergent and Convergent Thinking.

More on this in a bit but for now let's meet the forces for good and give a BIG shout out loud like we mean it hello to…

THE BEYONDERS

...BLACK DIAMOND

has a built-in compass to consistently navigate the competing challenges, **Fight the Right Foe**, outsmart and outmaneuver them. Most often it's not even a fair fight. He uses facts, data and logic to choose which foes to fight. He prioritizes the challenges that he has the energy, passion, expertise and resources to pursue, and those that will deliver the greatest impact. With his ability to laser focus he prevents expensive false starts that consume valuable time, resources and energy. To successfully **Fight the Right Foe**, he takes these **Key Actions**:

- **Explore the Challenge**
- **See the Future**
- **Get the Facts**
- **Clarify the Problem/Opportunity**

The outcomes are well clarified and prioritized challenges/problems/opportunities!

His *Powers* are:

- *Find It*
- *See It*
- *Be Versatile*

...MICRO-BURST

is revered for her explosive power to **Rain and Select Ideas** in short, compressed time periods. By collaborating with her sidekicks *Prism* and *Plusser*, she knows that by working together, **Imagination will Triumph**. She's a sprinter and gets out of the blocks mighty fast. She quickly transitions between novel divergent thinking to feasible convergent thinking, creating her own *momentum* in the process. Novelty and abundance are her trademarks as she uses four *white-hot* diverging principles to **Rain Ideas:**

- **Defer Judgment**
- **Make Quantity of Ideas Your Friend**
- **Build off, Combine, Piggyback and Synthesize Ideas**
- **Seek Wild and Unusual Ideas**

To ensure **Imagination will Triumph** she takes these **key actions:**

- **Rain and Select Ideas**

The outcome is an abundance of novel and feasible ideas to solve the prioritized challenges, problems or opportunities.

Her *Powers* are:

- *Be Fluent*
- *Be Novel*
- *Stay Open*

...PRISM

has the unique ability to **Take a Break and Incubate** on ideas, generate additional ones and put together new combinations. Being a student of physics, he has keen insight and realizes that ideas have varying frequencies and can flow and refract in different directions — to expand wide beyond current boundaries and to contract in between the lines. By integrating his ideas with those from his sidekick *Micro-Burst*, he develops a host of new idea combinations.

To ensure **Imagination will Triumph** he takes this **key action:**

- *Take a Break and Incubate*

The outcome is a set of new and revised idea combinations and alternatives to solve the prioritized challenges, problems or opportunities!

His *Powers* are:

- *Borrow It*
- *Elaborate*
- *Make New Connections*

...PLUSSER

takes the ideas generated by her sidekicks **Micro-Burst** and **Prism**, uses her unique **Power** to cobble them together into an actionable concept, and then **Strengthens the Concept** to be a Best Concept/ Prototype. She first finds the plusses and affirms the potential of the concept. Second, she employs *'goal wishing'* to identify the drawbacks of the concept. Third, she generates ideas to overcome or minimize the drawbacks. Only the strongest concepts move forward to ensure the highest probability of success.

To ensure **Imagination will Triumph** she takes this **key action:**

- *Strengthen the Concept*

The outcome is a Best Concept/Prototype that solves the prioritized challenge, problem or opportunity!

Her *Powers* are:

- *Put Ideas in Context*
- *Evaluate and Select It*
- *Strengthen It*

...*MOMENTUM*

is peerless in embodying *The Power of Speed*. He has an irrepressible bias for action to move ideas and concepts that are solid and viable forward to implementation. He is optimistic, intuitive and enjoys humor (especially his own). He tunes into what his head, heart and gut are telling him by staying versatile, learning and adapting quickly! Once a concept or prototype has passed the mustard test from his sidekick *Plusser*, he wastes virtually no time and advances it quickly. No time for delay, not now, not ever!

To ensure **The Power of Speed** he takes these **key actions:**

- **Xcelerate the Momentum**
- **Catapult the Energy**

The outcome is an implemented Best Concept/Prototype.

His *Powers* are:

- *Be Optimistic*
- *Use Humor and Intuition*
- *Act on It*

RESISTORS THAT INHIBIT OUR CREATIVE SPIRIT

It's not the mountain we conquer, but ourselves.

— New Zealand mountaineer Sir Edmund Hillary and
Sherpa mountaineer Tenzing Norgay
First climbers to reach the summit of Mount Everest

It certainly is noble to talk about rediscovering our creative spirit, strengthening our creativity muscle, increasing our productivity, anchoring creative habits and catapulting our best ideas to action. Sure, these are good outcomes, goals of what we want to happen. However, unlike in *The Wizard of Oz*, no one has built a yellow-brick road for us to skip along till we reach the Emerald City and meet up with the Great and Powerful Oz. **Resistors** to creativity are real (and perceived), they do exist, we face them every day and they can and do inhibit our natural creative productivity. Merriam-Webster defines *resistance* as refusal to accept something new or different. **Resistors** are internal and external barriers/blocks that impede and slow down our creative productivity and inhibit taking risks and positive action on our best ideas.

In collaboration with many great clients over the past twenty years I have worked to identify barriers that slow down and stifle creative productivity. I ask the foundational question, "***What's Stopping You***?" The question is powerful—it can stop you in your tracks—because when you think and get clear about the answers, you have effectively identified the **Resistors**. Aghghgh, sometimes they are visible, yet many other times they aren't. But they are always lurking in the shadows, they are most always present, and they need to be conquered.

Our challenge in conquering the **Resistors** is threefold:

- Shine the light on them—bright and wide.
- Call them out loud and clear, name them and laugh at them.
- Galvanize our energy and engage in proactive actions to significantly reduce their impact.

Or better yet, to eradicate them entirely from our thinking. This is by no means a tiny challenge. In fact it's big enough that to be victorious will require galvanizing and calling on our *B e y o n d e r Powers*. More on this in a bit, but the time has come; the time is now to meet these sneaky and very irritating **Resistors** *and to shine the light on them bright and wide.*

THE RESISTORS

THE DELAYERS

Personal Resistors

- Self-Doubt
- Rationalization
- Procrastination

If you want to get downright personal, then let's meet quite possibly the most stubborn and close to home **Resistor** of them all. One that is quite personal, don't you think? *'If only…I had gone for the gold… had the nerve and taken the risk…studied more…worked out more… been luckier and gotten the breaks…'* and the beat goes on, the beat goes on. These beats hit the nail right on the head because there is no one else to blame, no place to hide, really no good excuses. The *Personal Resistors* of **Self-Doubt, Rationalization and Procrastination** collaborate really well, taking us in the wrong direction. Together they are a debilitating *triple threat*!

The Delayers are in business because we are fallible human beings, heaping up a whole lot of *coulda, woulda, shoulda.* And we most likely have come down with a good ol' severe case of *The Gottas*—with a long list of *gotta, gotta dos*…that shield us from leveraging our creative strengths and hunting the good stuff! We can be awfully busy, making lists, multi-tasking with a whole *lotta gotta, gotta dos.* And while we will always be fallible, our goal here is to be a whole lot less fallible. You may very well want to change the beat, but **The Delayers** are continually scheming so that you don't change the damn beat. They don't want it to be the dawning of a new day…they don't want you to declare you aren't going to do it that way anymore…they want your good old days of **Self-Doubt, Rationalization and Procrastination** to continue and go on beating forever!

CHAMELEON

Rules, Traditions & Cultural Resistors

> - An Overemphasis of the Status-Quo
> - Social Influences and Conformity Pressures

Wikipedia defines chameleons as a distinctive and highly specialized clade of old world lizards with 202 species. These species abound in different colors and many have the ability to change colors.

Some species, such as Smith's dwarf chameleon, which live in South Africa, adjust their colors for camouflage in accordance with the vision of the specific bird or snake predator species that are threatening them. This adaptive capability is quite mandatory in the Reptilia world and has contributed to the staggering fact that chameleons have roamed the earth for at least 80 million years.

Switching from Reptilia to the world of Homo sapiens, when we are threatened, we should certainly borrow the chemical capacity of the Smith's dwarf chameleon and conform. But that's it! When you are overly concerned about preserving the status-quo and conforming, the norm is to:

- Follow all rules, traditions and customs that guide personal, team and organizational behavior.
- Go along to get along. Stay on your well-groomed trail, don't traverse into someone else's trail—or get in their 'sandbox.'
- Overemphasize status-quo thinking because it is *safe.*
- Prematurely criticize new ideas. After all, new ideas are far too *risky.*

Chameleon makes sure she conforms and fits in, keeps her head low, follows the rules, stays in her lane—her territory *where she is supposed to be* and doesn't challenge assumptions, the status-quo or why we do things the way we do. At a minimum, she sounds really boring...quite stifling in fact.

DAN COLEMAN

THE JUNK YARD DOG

Thinking and Perceiving Resistors

> • Thinking, Perceiving
>   and Responding in
>   Habit-Bound Ways.

The Junk Yard Dog barks long and loud at everybody and everything he isn't familiar with, doesn't recognize and doesn't know. Who the heck said variety is the spice of life? I must have been absent that day. Unless forced to do so, we become quite comfortable and accustomed to experiencing the world in predictable and non-enriching ways. We stay in our comfort zones, thank you. We perceive, think about, evaluate problems and ideas, and respond to people in very familiar ways. Consequently, *we experience little variance*, which is the lifeblood of creativity. *Varied and new stimuli spark novel thinking and perceiving.* Limited and homogenous stimuli are a very dull mixture. In craving predictability, we unwittingly block seeing new alternatives, applications, idea combinations, meanings, patterns, relationships and uses. We think, perceive and respond with limited imagination.

The Junk Yard Dog simply isn't interested in learning new ways of approaching problems or opportunities, or deviating from the routines and habits he has spent a good deal of time perfecting. He is a creature of habit in how he learns, goes through his day, interacts with people (*oh, he cherishes his checklists*). He learned the majority of what was needed way back in grammar school: write down what the teacher says, don't really question it, memorize it, speak only when called on and study by the book. No need for any experiential, guided discovery or reflective learning methods here. Just the way the world is supposed to work, according to the script of this highly structured and habit-bound **Resistor**!

THE 3 HEADED GREMLIN

Emotional Resistors

> - Fear of Failure
> - Fear of Ambiguity
> - Fear of Rejection

The 3 Headed Gremlin is certainly a sly, secretive and slippery **Resistor**. Most always present and frequently not talked about (can't talk about fear; that would be too real). Many relationships and team collaboration problems have their origins rooted in the need for power, control and status hierarchy—with fear close by. The **Emotional Resistors** play out very deviously:

- *If I must win, I fear failing*—or someone else winning, or even worse yet, someone else getting the credit. Translation: only play the games you know you can win—the easier, safe ones. Paired together, if I must be right, I fear being wrong. *Playing not to lose vs. playing to win here?* Probably not uncovering any new terrain or discoveries with this puppy.

- *If I must be in control, I fear ambiguity*. Does anyone else see a good, old-fashioned turf battle brewing on the horizon with this one? No need for any substantive, cross-functional collaboration here.

- *If I must fit in, I fear rejection*. And yes, I am a team player (or at least want to give the *appearance* of being a team player). If we're wearing green uniforms and I have a purple idea, I'll take one for the team and let go of that purple idea—only green ones are welcome here. Now that you mention it, I never really liked purple much in the first place.

Is it an understatement to say these three *Fatal Fears* stymie creativity and innovation? You caught me; that was a pseudo question (a statement disguised as a question). I'm just attempting to appear to be a good team player here.

DAN COLEMAN

THE VICE

Workplace Pressure Resistors

> - Extreme Time Pressures
> - Unrealistic Expectations for Creative Productivity
> - Distractions from Creative Work

It sure would have been more profitable if I had collected a shiny silver dollar every time someone said to me, "Dan, these creative-thinking practices and tools are interesting BUT I live in the real world and I think you only visit it from time to time. I just don't have the luxury of time on my side to think about new ideas. I've got to focus on the fundamentals, the blocking and tackling, and I can't be distracted from my day job."

And the beat goes on…the beat goes on. All of those shiny silver dollars sure would be weighing me down right now.

The Vice and his *Workload Pressure Resistors* are in play, most places, big time! **Extreme Time Pressures, Unrealistic Expectations for Creative Productivity and Distractions from Creative Work** are darn good, logical-sounding rationales; so good they are quite rational and believable. After all, people are quite busy doing the work they are paid to do, and with all the distractions *who the heck has got time to be creative? Just not enough hours in the day*! And to be held accountable for novel thinking and creative output? *Not volunteering for that one, no way, not now, not ever.* Well-meaning smart people will look you straight in the eye, not flinch, and give you a boldfaced proclamation, oftentimes using a self-righteous and indignant tone to boot. *"If only there were more hours in the day; If only I wasn't so busy; If only there weren't so many distractions."* If ifs and buts were berries and nuts we'd all have a Merry Christmas! Who the heck brought the fruit cake? Maybe you've met some of these people yourself—hmmm?

Ahh yes, **The Vice** gets us in his iron grasp and squeezes us hard twice; first, he steals our precious time for creativity and then gives us logical-sounding excuses to boot. And speaking of time, it's time to get to **Episode i.**

EPISODE I
FIGHT THE RIGHT FOE

THE TIME IS NOW

The chance will stand before you only once.

— Sandra Day O'Connor, former associate justice of the
Supreme Court of the United States

When we **Fight the Right Foe**, we *zero in on and identify the Challenge/ Dream.* In essence, a primary **Foe** is a list of good and worthy challenges, problems or opportunities we could spend our valuable time and resources on. However, *they are not necessarily the best or right one(s)* for you. We're not talking about small potatoes here or focused on incremental and modest goals. On the contrary, life's greatest accomplishments are fueled by a *DREAM.* There is nothing more powerful than the magnetic pull of a *DREAM.* When we are truly zeroed in on it and are fully motivated and committed to realizing the *DREAM*, it cannot be taken from us; it cannot be broken and cannot be beaten. When we **Fight the Right Foe**, we move purposely forward toward our *DREAM* and don't become distracted by other shiny objects, competing interests or other foes.

This is analogous to the sport of mountain climbing. The world offers many diverse mountains to climb and each mountain has its unique adventures, obstacles and risks. Each imposes demands on the skill, preparation and experience of each climber and team that attempts to reach its summit. Reaching the summit provides satisfaction and rewards for each climber and expedition team. However, it isn't feasible to attempt to climb a large number of mountains. They have to choose which one is the right one for them to climb. **Fight the Right Foe** and Climb the Right mountain are on the same side of the coin; they are interchangeable.

Therein lies the good fight. We can't be scattered, unfocused or undisciplined with our time and other vital resources because it's paramount to be clear on our summit. When we put ourselves in the place of highest potential, we make our own luck and we *see the right summit.* We are then positioned to map out the best routes to get there as efficiently as possible. Each mountain has its own topography and facts to study and consider. Similarly, *different Challenges/Dreams* have varying degrees of adventure, difficulty, risk—and payoff. We need to select the one(s) that are right for each of us. We don't have the time or the resources *to Fight the*

Wrong Foe and let them sap our precious energy, optimism, enthusiasm or determination.

Sure, there are obstacles (real and perceived) that stand between where we are right now and where we want to go. ***Self-Doubt, Rationalization and Procrastination*** stand at the front of the line. Got it! How about today we adopt a new fight song that goes something like this: **That was then, now is now!** What do you say? Let's unleash your *Black Diamond Powers* and *Lean into Risk, Embrace your Dream* and *Take Proactive Actions to go get it.*

However, **The Delayers** delight in wanting us to *Fight the Wrong Foe* for two reasons:

- It is their mission to prevent us—*to delay us* (possibly forever) from zeroing in on, *embracing* our *Dream/Big Goal/Shining Star/Wish*—what we really want to accomplish!
- They can infiltrate our creative spirit if we let them. They unleash three debilitating forces to undermine our creativity and do everything in their power to get us to *Fight the Wrong Foe:*

  - **Self-Doubt**
  - **Rationalization**
  - **Procrastination**

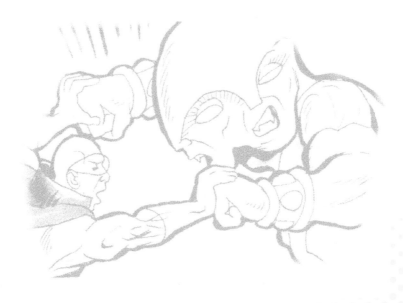

SELF-DOUBT

If you think you can fall, you're more likely to.

— Nick Wallenda, acrobat, high wire aerialist and daredevil

In my workshops I ask the participants, *"Who here sees themselves as creative?"* Sadly, far too few people raise their hands. The unfortunate reality is many people don't see themselves as creative because they believe creativity is the sole domain of the arts: artists, writers, musicians and comics. And yes, the arts certainly have a good market share of highly talented and creative people, and so do many other professions including education, business, medicine, counseling, and raising a family to name a few.

A better question is, *"In what ways does your creativity surface?"* You have a natural capacity to generate novel ideas *and to act on them.* I will continue to stress this central point and another point is to *get them out of your head, on paper and catapult them forward!* **Smell my vapor fumes, baby!** A nasty thief that chips away at our confidence daily and fans the flames of self-doubt is our *Internal Voice of Judgment.*

Internal Voice of Judgment (IVOJ)

Comedian Groucho Marx began his career in the 1920s and made people laugh with his slapstick comedy routines. He had snappy one-liners and a sharp wit, always poking fun at himself. Groucho's comedy routine could have made him the poster child of self-doubting our ability to be creative, e.g. **The Groucho Marx** brainstorming method. It would go something like this:

"How could it be a good idea? I thought of it."
"If it's such a good idea, somebody else would have thought about it already."

Using his comedy as a metaphor, the Groucho Marx brainstorming method personifies our *IVOJ*—the voice in our heads that tells us not to move forward with an idea or initiative and says things like:

"It'll never work!"	"Quit dreaming and get practical!"	"No one would ever want to buy it!"
"Where will you get the funding?"	"Keep your head low!"	"Don't rock the boat!"
"You have a family to support!"	"You can't pay for your children's college education on a whim!"	"I've never been that creative!"

One cause of self-doubt is our perception of new ideas contrasted to what we know. We often perceive existing ideas and ways of doing things to be good and we perceive new ideas with suspicion. Why is this? One cause is that existing ideas and ways of doing things conform to our *existing nine dots of reference and experience* because we recognize them. Big, new ideas challenge our status-quo thinking because they fall outside of our nine dots frame of reference and experience. Essentially, they disrupt our expectations and our world view. As a result, we often view them as *bad* because we are not familiar enough with them. Old, nasty self-doubt is rearing its homely head again.

The ability to laugh at one's self is a strength; however, when the *IVOJ* rears its ugly head, it becomes a debilitating force and pushes against our creative productivity. It can prevent you from moving forward, but only if you let it. And if that isn't enough to raise the anxiety level of self-doubt, how about we take it up a notch or two and add to it the *External Voice of Judgment?*

External Voice of Judgment (EVOJ)

If our *IVOJ* wasn't potent enough, the *EVOJ* is alive and well. Many people audition for this part and are ready willing and able (bless their hearts) to share their well-meaning criticisms about your ideas and concepts. This really helps us to put the brakes on. Speed bumps have always irked me. Who is the knucklehead who put that one here?

Taking a brief look back at American history, many new ideas were met with resistance, even ridicule. The bigger the idea the greater the resistance. People generally don't like big, new ideas until they prove to be successful. A few startling, incorrect predictions:

Everything that can be invented has been invented.

— Charles Duell, Director of U.S. Patent Office, 1899

Sensible and responsible women do not want to vote.

— President Grover Cleveland, 1905

Who the hell wants to hear actors talk?

— Harry Warner, Warner Brothers Pictures, 1927

There is a worldwide market for about five computers.

— Thomas Watson, President of IBM, 1949

We don't like their sound and guitar music is on the way out.

— Decca Recording Company on declining to sign the Beatles, 1962

There's no chance that the iPhone is going to gain any significant market share.

— Steve Ballmer, Microsoft CEO, 2007

Following are my seven favorite (not) *EVOJ Personalities*. My guess is you have previously met many of these people:

- **The Bottom Liner** without missing a beat will parrot back their blather of, "it's not in the budget; let's get back to basics; it's time for lean and mean; we don't have the resources; and cost out at any cost." This appears to be quite pragmatic on the surface but isn't.

- **The Yes Butter** is sly with their false praise to include phrases like, "It's such a fabulous idea, but…" and of course, once you hear *but* everything before *the but* just got dismissed.

- **The Pushy Pragmatist** with their sleight-of-hand, logical-appearing commentary that "the operations people won't go for it." Sure, trying to save us from pursuing something that just won't happen.

- **The Salty Old Sage** pretends to be on your side, yet they don't let you forget this isn't their first rodeo and want to keep you from making the same mistakes they made before electricity was discovered.

- **The Doomsayer** wouldn't know a good idea if it bit them in the you know what, but they will sure tell you what's wrong with your idea and how the world as we now know it will come to an end if you persist.

- **The Bring Back the Good Old Day-ser** longingly waits for the present to pass—it surely will—and the good old days will return so we can get back to normal and deal with this the way we always used to.

- **The Grinner** will look you directly in the eye and with a straight face tell you a bold-face lie because it is what they think you want to hear. Without missing a beat after you've left, continue to do what they have always done with no intention of adopting your idea.

The *IVOJ & EVOJ* are debilitating forces that contribute to self-doubting our capacity to consistently generate novel thinking…only if we let them!

RATIONALIZATION

*Only remember west of the Mississippi it's a little more look, see, act.
A little less rationalize, comment, talk.*

— F. Scott Fitzgerald, American novelist

Merriam-Webster defines rationalization as, *"to think about or describe something (such as bad behavior) in a way that explains it and makes it seem proper, more attractive."* It can be insidious. Not only can we rationalize just about anything, we can also rationalize why we rationalize. Now try to rationalize that! For example, *"I wasn't born creative, heck, my parents weren't creative, and the fruit doesn't fall far from the tree. You don't get avocados when you plant potatoes."* Many children weren't encouraged to be creative at a young age, and that's where habits and interests are formed. I can be darned creative when I can come up with some really good whoppers rationalizing why I don't think creatively, and why my creative production is anemic. If you don't see and think of yourself as being creative, this thinking becomes a self-fulfilling prophecy. This prophecy plays out similarly to how the ladder of inference (Senge, 1994) works. If I don't see myself as creative my self-fulfilling prophecy begins on the bottom rung of the ladder and climbs upward, and I basically only look for data that supports and reinforces my self-fulfilling prophecy.

The Ladder of Inference

We go through life not testing our assumptions, biases or beliefs. We reach conclusions based on what we observe and infer from our experience. By not taking time out to challenge these conclusions we are prone to replicate patterns of behavior. These patterns are so imbedded in our thinking that if unchecked we can believe that *our views and beliefs are accurate. Our views and beliefs are based on facts. The facts that we have selected are real and true. And this is quite obvious.*

So as a result, if I don't see myself as creative...

- I take actions based on my belief about how things are.
- I adopt and reinforce beliefs about how things are.
- I reach conclusions.
- I make certain assumptions based on the meanings I have added.
- I think about what I observe and add meaning to the data.
- I have experiences, observe and record data.
- I select data from my interpretation of what I observe.

At the root of this thinking is the anxiety associated with uncertainty, of not knowing and the social pressure of needing to have our ideas accepted. Thinking positively, if you provide yourself with reassurance and affirmation, it helps to alleviate both fears of uncertainty and acceptance of one's ideas.

PROCRASTINATION

You make your mistakes to get to the good stuff.

— Quincy Jones, jazz musician, producer and composer

Procrastination is the **Personal Resistor** that most everyone can relate to. Merriam-Webster defines procrastination as, *"to put off intentionally and habitually; be slow or late about doing something that should be done; to delay until a later time because you do not want to do it."* It is quite devious, especially when working with its cohort, **Rationalization**. It's not that we don't want to generate novel ideas for our business, life, and family. We simply say, *"gonna, gonna do that tomorrow."* It sounds so rational. The nonproductive habits of the **Personal Resistors** are tricky to counteract, yet procrastination may be in a class by itself. The crime isn't that we put some things off until tomorrow or next week, it's that sometimes *we put them off for a lifetime.* And when we're sitting on our deathbed it's too late if we procrastinate our life away (ouch!). One reason we procrastinate is to avoid or postpone some form of pain. If, for example, I need to generate some novel ideas, there can be pain associated with that—fear of drawing blanks; of not having imaginative ones; of being questioned about them; of having to decide on them; of having to take a different course of action. So, I put it off. No need to feel that pain today—or anytime soon for that matter!

Another cause of procrastination is that we frame things too big, e.g., national health care, writing a book this weekend, generating 50 ideas in five minutes to solve a problem. These are too big to solve, so why start? You don't roll out national health care, you start with a component like focusing on prevention. You don't write a book, you write three pages a day. You don't generate 50 ideas in five minutes; you begin by generating 15 ideas and build from there.

When in the throes of everyday life, we are busy accomplishing the tasks directly in front of us, getting things done today, this week. It is somewhat rational to put off or delay thinking about or taking action on our life's dream. Heck, I may not have even clarified what the dream is, let alone take steps to pursue it. It just seems to be out of reach right now and not practical to focus on. I am quite busy, and I tell myself there will be time for it, just not now. And I pat myself on the back for being practical and put my head back down to tackle the pile of stuff that is right in front of me, seemingly demanding my attention.

RED PIN BOWLING ANYONE?

Say hello to **Two-Board Adjustments.** Their purpose is to help anchor creative thinking as a repeatable habit. Growing up 30 miles south of the Canadian border, the winters were long and cold, so to take it on we skied, skated, played basketball and bowled. Of all the sports I found bowling demanded that you make small adjustments in real time. Each lane has 39 one-inch boards between the left and right gutters, with board #20 in the center and the center arrow and dot placed on it. Each arrow and dot to the left and right is placed on the fifth board from board #20. This means there are three arrows and dots on each side of the center arrow and dot, spaced about five inches apart from each other, providing a close-in target to aim at.

In a match, each team of five bowlers share two lanes, bowling on alternating lanes every other frame. The two lanes often have varying lane conditions (e.g., one lane hooks more, requiring adjusting the ball speed; using different balls made from various materials to grip the lane; or aiming at another lane arrow). You learn to adjust your approach to the lane conditions *now* because it will be the fifth frame and you will be sucking eggs. Making small adjustments early is the difference between winning and losing (and also having a little luck with the crossover Brooklyn strikes, my specialty).

And speaking of not self-doubting, rationalizing and procrastinating, how about we summon and enlist *The B e y o n d e r* who is uniquely qualified to conquer **The Delayers** and any other **Resistor** that may try to pile on for that matter...

MAKE A TWO-BOARD ADJUSTMENT

Develop and Implement Daily Tests

Ask, "What is the specific skill or technique I'm trying to isolate to improve, to perfect?"
"How best to measure it?"
"How to make a game of it?"

...*BLACK DIAMOND*

is consistently able to **Fight the Right Foe**
by taking these **Key Actions:**

- **Explore the Challenge**
- **See the Future**
- **Get the Facts**
- **Clarify the Problem/ Opportunity**

   With a built-in navigation compass,
he stays zeroed in on the current, real-time challenges, problems or opportunities and avoids costly stops and starts. His legendary focus is unmatched in the modern era. The outcomes are well clarified challenges, problems or opportunities!

   His *Powers* are:

Find It

- Define a variety of challenges/problems/opportunities that could be pursued or solved.
- Find many problems/opportunities, uncover missing or incomplete information and zero in on the most pertinent facts.
- Analyze and clarify various elements of problems and opportunities.
- Demonstrate genuine curiosity and ask insightful and provocative questions.

See It

- Fantasize about things that don't yet exist.
- Use vivid and varied mental imagery to see the future.
- Identify potential barriers that could prevent achieving a future vision.
- Draw a sharp distinction between the present and future vision to create a tension that stimulates proactive action.

Be Versatile

- Use different approaches to problem-solving.
- Simplify problems/opportunities without losing essential details.
- View problems/opportunities through various lenses, different frames.
- Persevere when facing complex or ambiguous issues and problems.

EXPLORE THE CHALLENGE

By endurance, we conquer.

— Ernest Shackleton, polar explorer

To successfully **Fight the Right Foe**, it's paramount to gain crystal clarity on *the Challenge/Dream that we really want to embrace, reach for and accomplish.* Oliver Wendell Holmes, Jr. (2020), an American poet, said:

> *"Many people die with their music still in them. Too often it is because they are always getting ready to live. Before they know it, time runs out."*

Dying with our music inside us sounds morbid, kind of a drag. That's not what we want. Professor William Purkey (2020), author and professor at the University of North Carolina Greensboro, is credited with coining the phrases: *"You gotta dance like there's nobody watching; love like you'll never be hurt; sing like there's nobody listening;* and *live like it's heaven on earth."* Yes, that's the attitude! Find your music, reach way down into your belly, pull it up and belt it out time after time! And if you are a little off key, who cares? Sing even louder!

A good $64,000 question is, *"What is the Challenge/Dream* I should reach for and pursue?" Sometimes it's obvious, staring us in the face. Other times it's not as clear, and there appears to be a seductive number of worthy *Challenges/Dreams* to chase, reach and wish for. We don't have the passion, time, resources or expertise to chase them all, let alone even a few of them. Therein lies the point. We have to identify, explore and prioritize the *best one(s).* In his book, *Good to Great,* Jim Collins (2001) argued that *good* is the enemy of *great.* There are a number of good challenges to go after, however far fewer great ones. If we find ourselves spending precious time and energy just chasing the good ones, we will never summon enough courage, resources and energy to go after the big ones.

And it's quite seductive to be in a constant state of motion, like the Tasmanian Devil constantly whirling like a tornado, very busy multitasking and proud of it. This has the trappings of equating being busy and efficient with being productive and effective. Being busy does not equal being productive. It is a far lower score. Being productive is a good thing, but that isn't really all that energizing. It isn't the real deal either. How about we take the elevator up to the 103rd floor of the Empire State Building! How about we *Lean into Risk! Embrace and Chase our Dream! Pursue*

Happiness (wasn't there a movie about that?)! Be Really Prosperous! Strive for Great! Become Fulfilled! Reach for your Bright Shining Star! 'Leave it all on the Field'! Now we're talking real turkey; we're cooking with gas and firing on all 16 cylinders! When you **Explore the Challenge** you go after, reach for and embrace *your Challenge/Dream and Take Proactive Actions to go get it*! You can't hit a round-tripper if you're slapping for singles! Nor can you drive a spike with a tack hammer!

SEE THE FUTURE

Every great dream begins with a dreamer. Always remember,
you have within you the strength, the patience
and the passion to reach for the stars, to change.

— Harriet Tubman, abolitionist, conductor on the Underground Railroad

Author Lewis Carroll (2020) said, "*If you don't know where you are going, any road will get you there.*" **Black Diamond** takes the output from *Explore the Challenge* and puts in the effort to *See It,* to see the desired future he is genuinely excited about. He is restless with the gap that exists between current reality and the future vision. To *See It* you produce a visual image of the journey that is possible by putting yourself in the place of greatest potential. You create your own luck. You cannot accomplish big feats without a big idea; you can't sustain a strong ascent without a solid trail guide; and you can't fully harness your energy without first *Seeing It*. In essence, you transport yourself *to the future,* to where you want to be, and look at the past, which is the present of course. You then see and tell the tale of the journey you took. You want a clear view of your destination and ensure you are genuinely excited about the vision and all of its possibilities.

And it is emotions first baby! It's about being emotionally engaged and *then the logic will follow in good time*. It's unbridled energy…*live steam.* How 'bout going for a ride to the ocean in my vintage Jaguar? Heck, it's only a few hundred miles away. If the energy regenerates and your heart is still racing, then and only then do you engage the logic and outline the steps necessary to achieve your vision. You have to have a *really hot vision*, because if you don't, it's inevitable the flame will flicker and then go out. The climb will become too intense and you will tire. You will become too distracted. You won't grow dissatisfied nearly enough with your current reality. With a *really hot vision* full of possibilities and belief in being able to achieve it, you've created a powerful magnet where you are pulled forward to get going and bridge the gap between where you are and where you want to be! In his book, *The Path of Least Resistance,* Robert Fritz (1994) described **creative tension** as an intense tension between your current reality and your destination that compels you to take the action, to lean into risk. With creative tension you have seen it and experienced the journey you now need to take! **Time marches on and waits for no one!**

GET THE FACTS

The important thing is not to stop questioning. Curiosity has its own reason for existing. One cannot help but be in awe when he/she contemplates the mysteries of eternity, of life, of the marvelous structure of reality. It is enough if one tries merely to comprehend a little of this mystery every day. Never lose your curiosity.

— Albert Einstein, Nobel Prize winning physicist

In the TV show *Dragnet,* Sgt. Joe Friday, a detective in the Los Angeles, CA police department, is well-remembered for one of his famous lines: "*Just the facts, ma'am.*" Except that isn't factually accurate. What he actually said was, "*All we want are the facts, ma'am.*" Minor detail, and the essence is the same.

After **Seeing It, Black Diamond** does not become distracted by shiny new objects. He is a cool operator and prefers to get **Just the Facts** (data, details, information and facts). He is clear-eyed on the destination, the summit, **The Right Foe**. The challenge at hand is to discover the important data, facts, details and information required for a successful ascent. There often are a variety of trails and tactics available to navigate the journey. Data and facts come from a variety of sources including literature reviews, interviews, excursions, new observations and experiments. It's important to develop a solid data collection plan to cast a wide enough net, yet not so wide to boil the ocean.

Logical, methodical *and also versatile* in his approach, he is adroit at maintaining his balance, cool and composed when confronted with ambiguity, new information or complexity. He discerns the critical information and facts early on and discards those that are tangential and of little importance. Based on what he learns, he may need to adapt, ask revised questions or adjust the plan by integrating specialized resources, modifying the timeline or reallocating financial resources.

With the facts in hand, *Black Diamond* zeros in to **Clarify the Right Problem/Opportunity**. Every problem and opportunity have unique characteristics and it's critical to choose the ones that suit the interests, skills, resources and energy of the explorer. Ideas follow the way problems/opportunities are framed. That's why it's important to frame them wide, narrow and in-between—and then choose the ones to pursue that, when solved, will deliver the greatest impact.

CLARIFY THE RIGHT PROBLEM/OPPORTUNITY

If we spend our time climbing the ladder, and we find out when we get to the top that the ladder is not leaning against the right wall, every step we took just got us to the wrong place faster.

— Stephen Covey, author of *The 7 Habits of Highly Successful People*

APPROXIMATE AND PRECISE THINKING

Merriam-Webster defines *approximate* as, *"early correct, close in value or amount but not precise."* *Precise* is defined as *"exactly or precisely defined or stated; minutely exact."* As a rule of thumb, we are often better served to be approximate early on in problem finding and clarifying, and to generate many *approximately right* problem statements. This is especially true when it isn't apparent what is the *exact problem* to solve or opportunity to pursue. Frame the problems in unique ways and look at them through different lenses (narrow, broad and in-between). We need to be more discriminating and precise downstream because errors later on are darn expensive (*i.e., solving the wrong problem, that's expensive!*). With precise thinking we look to *define the right problem, the right opportunity, the right answer and the right solution.* It's not an either/or decision, it's more of a both/and/when decision. There is an ongoing tug of war tension between precise thinking and approximate thinking. So, think approximate until precision is required and meaningful. Insistence on precision too early eliminates all except exact matches. Similar to playing poker, the key is to have the insight and wisdom to know which card to play, and when. Kenny Rogers had it right when he sang, *"You gotta know when to hold 'em, know when to fold 'em, know when to walk away, know when to run."*

MAKE A TWO-BOARD ADJUSTMENT

Establish Weekly
Problem-Finding Quotas

Sales managers use selling quotas to motivate people. In my programs I ask my audience, "If you are in sales, and going to a sales meeting and aren't at quota, what do you need at a minimum?" The answer that tickles me most is, "a damn good story." Let's borrow the use of quotas to increase our productivity by establishing a weekly problem statement or question quota. Hold yourself accountable to meet it and don't make it too easy. Also, don't make it so arduous that it brings non-productive pressure on you. I find generating 20 problem statements or questions weekly against a challenge is a workable quota.

Yes and speaking of having no time, the time has come for **Black Diamond** to use his **Powers** in **Battle #1** because he has no time for **The Delayers**...or **The 3 Headed Gremlin!**

BATTLE #1

...BLACK DIAMOND HAS NO TIME FOR THE DELAYERS

His **Powers** are:

- *Find It*
- *See It*
- *Be Versatile*

Personal Resistors

- **Self-Doubt**
- **Rationalization**
- **Procrastination**

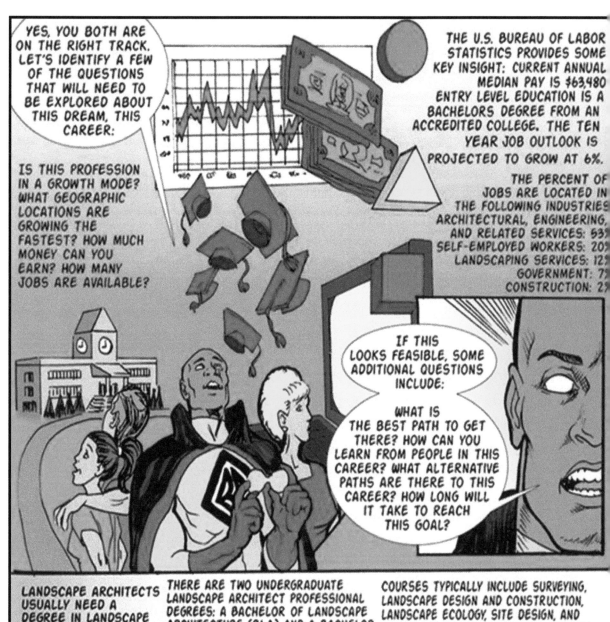

YES, YOU BOTH ARE ON THE RIGHT TRACK. LET'S IDENTIFY A FEW OF THE QUESTIONS THAT WILL NEED TO BE EXPLORED ABOUT THIS DREAM, THIS CAREER:

IS THIS PROFESSION IN A GROWTH MODE? WHAT GEOGRAPHIC LOCATIONS ARE GROWING THE FASTEST? HOW MUCH MONEY CAN YOU EARN? HOW MANY JOBS ARE AVAILABLE?

THE U.S. BUREAU OF LABOR STATISTICS PROVIDES SOME KEY INSIGHT: CURRENT ANNUAL MEDIAN PAY IS $63,480 ENTRY LEVEL EDUCATION IS A BACHELORS DEGREE FROM AN ACCREDITED COLLEGE. THE TEN YEAR JOB OUTLOOK IS PROJECTED TO GROW AT 6%.

THE PERCENT OF JOBS ARE LOCATED IN THE FOLLOWING INDUSTRIES ARCHITECTURAL, ENGINEERING, AND RELATED SERVICES: 53% SELF-EMPLOYED WORKERS: 20% LANDSCAPING SERVICES: 12% GOVERNMENT: 7% CONSTRUCTION: 2%

IF THIS LOOKS FEASIBLE, SOME ADDITIONAL QUESTIONS INCLUDE:

WHAT IS THE BEST PATH TO GET THERE? HOW CAN YOU LEARN FROM PEOPLE IN THIS CAREER? WHAT ALTERNATIVE PATHS ARE THERE TO THIS CAREER? HOW LONG WILL IT TAKE TO REACH THIS GOAL?

LANDSCAPE ARCHITECTS USUALLY NEED A DEGREE IN LANDSCAPE ARCHITECTURE AND A STATE-ISSUED LICENSE, WHICH TYPICALLY REQUIRES COMPLETION OF AN INTERNSHIP.

THERE ARE TWO UNDERGRADUATE LANDSCAPE ARCHITECT PROFESSIONAL DEGREES: A BACHELOR OF LANDSCAPE ARCHITECTURE (BLA) AND A BACHELOR OF SCIENCE IN LANDSCAPE ARCHITECTURE (BSLA). THESE PROGRAMS USUALLY REQUIRE 4 TO 5 YEARS OF STUDY.

COURSES TYPICALLY INCLUDE SURVEYING, LANDSCAPE DESIGN AND CONSTRUCTION, LANDSCAPE ECOLOGY, SITE DESIGN, AND URBAN AND REGIONAL PLANNING, HISTORY OF LANDSCAPE ARCHITECTURE, PLANT AND SOIL SCIENCE, GEOLOGY, PROFESSIONAL PRACTICE, AND GENERAL MANAGEMENT.

EPISODE PROFILE:
DR. JANE GOODALL

*What you do makes a difference,
and you've got to decide what kind of difference you want to make.*

— Dr. Jane Goodall, Primatologist

Merriam-Webster defines trailblazer as "*a person who makes, does, or discovers something new and makes it acceptable.*" Say hello to a true trailblazer!

Her story has been told many times, and like a fine wine, it doesn't grow old, it only gets better with age. Dr. Goodall conducted scientific research on chimpanzees in Africa in the 1960s and

Source, National Geographic

revolutionized primate science. Her discoveries negated firmly held beliefs about chimpanzees, humankind's closest living relatives. In 1960 Dr. Goodall began her field research at the Gombe Stream Chimpanzee Reserve in western Tanzania where she made groundbreaking discoveries that were in direct opposition to the scientific community's accepted beliefs about chimpanzees:

1. *They eat meat:* She observed chimps eating a bush pig and attacking, killing and eating a red colobus monkey. Prior to this it was thought they were vegetarians.

2. *They make and use tools:* She observed David Greybeard (she recorded observations of the chimps by names she gave them) using a blade of grass to catch termites from their mounds and removing leaves from a twig to use it to fish for termites.

These discoveries forced the scientific community to acknowledge that humans weren't the only *Homo sapiens* to make and use tools. At Gombe,

55

she persevered through natural threats, including malaria, parasites, snakes and storms. When she published her field research it was met with harsh skepticism by the male-dominated primatologist community:

- After presenting her findings at the Zoological Society of London's primate symposium in 1962, one society officer criticized her work as *"anecdotal and speculative that made no real contribution to science."*
- An Associated Press reporter wrote, *"A willowy blonde with more time for monkeys than men told how she spent fifteen months in the jungle to study the habits of the apes."*

Media executives hinged their support on her cooperation to be glamorized and scripted. One *National Geographic* executive wrote, *"Good shots of Jane washing her hair in a stream would be a big help."* If it served to sustain her work, she made sacrifices, humored fools, endured slights, made concessions and persevered. In 1965 *National Geographic* published its first cover story about her work and released *Miss Goodall and the Wild Chimpanzees* as a television special that highlighted the lives of chimps. An estimated 22 million North American viewers tuned in to see it. She continued her field research into the mid-1970s.

Since then, Dr. Goodall has authored dozens of books, spoken at hundreds of conferences and been a tireless ambassador in developing countries for animal protection, conservation, science and education. In 1977, she founded the Jane Goodall Institute to expand ways to create chimpanzee protection, conservation and environmental education. In 1986, Dr. Goodall shifted her focus to an animal-human conservation approach with the global mission: *to empower people to make a difference for all living things, for a future of green.*

The initiatives implemented include youth programs, a chimpanzee sanctuary and rehabilitation center, community conservation, science work and action plans. In 2017 the Institute celebrated its 40th anniversary, and noted the following accomplishments:

- 1490k+ acres of habitat protected
- 5000+ chimpanzees and gorillas living in the habitats
- JGI protects 130 communities supported worldwide

- 4900+ projects led by young people through Jane Goodall's Roots & Shoots

Pay Attention to Your Unique Calling: *Think Big, Lean into Risk, Embrace Your Dream and Take Proactive Actions to go get it*! Persevere, never let it go or ever give up. Take the actions for the long run. You will encounter tough obstacles, naysayers, hostilities, quicksand and inclement weather. You have a number of options to include: charm them; kill them with kindness; barrel over them; collaborate with them; outsmart them; or outrun them. They will tire, you won't! What is the *Dream* that is in you? The one you need to go after with every passionate and enthusiastic fiber in your body?

MAKE A TWO-BOARD ADJUSTMENT

Anticipate Hitting a Plateau

Don't be surprised or dissapointed when this happens because it will. Plan in advance what to do and how you are going to shift when you hit a plateau. We get stuck when we go on autopilot and simply go through the routines. Change your practice methods (e.g., speed up the repetitions, slow them down, do them in reverse, adapt them).

IT'S YOUR TIME

In the comic strip *Black Diamond* used his *Powers* of *Find It, See It* and *Be Versatile* to **Explore the Challenge, See the Future, Get the Facts** and **Clarify the Problem/Opportunity.** He helped Jessica and her parents **Fight the Right Foe,** clarify the right problem/opportunity and leave **The Delayers** and **The 3 Headed Gremlin** in their vapor fumes baby!

It's your time to channel your energy, your powerhouse. When you start strong you finish strong. By taking this trailblazing step and *working out* with **Dare to Dream, Back to the Future, Just the Facts Please, Reframe It,** and **Evaluate and Select 'Em** you will be well on your way to *Lean into Risk, Embrace Your Dream and Take Proactive Actions to go get it!*

EPISODE I, FIGHT THE RIGHT FOE: BATTLE #1

BURST IN HERE WHEN...

You want a new way to improve, create or solve something and need to explore the data, details, facts and emotion surrounding the challenge, problem or opportunity that requires your attention....

AND FIGHT OFF THE DELAYERS...

- Self Doubt
- Rationalization
- Procrastination

POWER SOURCES

- Dream
- Big Goal
- Shining Star
- Wish

THE DELAYERS   ...BLACK DIAMOND

VS.

POWERS

- Find It
- See It
- Be Versatile

KEY ACTIONS

- Explore the Challenge
- See the Future
- Get the Facts
- Clarify the Problem or Opportunity

WORKOUTS

- Dare to Dream
- Back to the Future
- Just the Facts Please
- Reframe It
- Evaluate and Select 'Em

OUTCOMES

CLARIFIED/PRIORITIZED PROBLEM/OPPORTUNITY STATEMENTS

FIGHT THE RIGHT FOE

EXPLORE THE CHALLENGE

Burst in here when…you want a new way to improve, create or solve something, and you need to explore the data, details and emotions surrounding the challenge/opportunity/problem that requires your attention.

⒟IVERGENT WORKOUT

DARE TO DREAM

When you **Dare to Dream** you diverge and leverage the strength and power of your dream. You wish for big things, set high goals, reach for that shining star and zero in on what matters most in your life! Take advantage of the westerly winds at your back and ask bold, provocative questions. Use the questions that follow to help chart your path forward!

Challenge/Dream Questions

What is your boldest, most daring dream?	Deep down, what is your life purpose?

As you think about your future vision…	What are your goals?
…What is your head saying to you?	Personal?
…What is your heart saying to you?	Professional?
…What is your gut saying to you?	Relationships?
	Financial?
Looking back on your life, when were you the happiest/most energized? What were you doing that was so enriching? How can you re-stoke those fires?	What are you uniquely talented at, love to do and should be doing most of the time?

List Your Dream/Big Goal/Shining Star/Wish Statements
'My Dream is…' 'My Big Goal is…' 'It Would be Great if…' 'I Wish…'

Converge, prioritize the best ones and put a check next to the ones that:

- Appeal to your head, tug at your heartstrings and kick you in the gut.
- Will demand novel thinking and are possible to achieve with a good stretch.
- You have ownership and decision-making authority.
- You are highly enthusiastic, motivated and energized to take bold, decisive action.

Bring your prioritized Dream/Big Goal/Shining Star/Wish Statements forward to **See the Future!**

FIGHT THE RIGHT FOE

SEE THE FUTURE

Burst in here when…you have prioritized your Dream/Big Goal/Shining Star/Wish Statements and want to see, feel and touch an ideal solution. Note: there is some overlap between the **Dare to Dream** and **Back to the Future Workouts**. The primary distinction is with **Dare to Dream** you visualize from the present to the future, and with **Back to the Future** you visualize from the future back to the present. In the comic strip we primarily used **Dare to Dream**, however one scene utilized **Back to the Future**

where Jessica saw her fate (courtesy of **The 3 Headed Gremlin** fanning fear). You can *work out* with both **Workouts** or use one in lieu of the other.

ⒹIVERGENT WORKOUT

BACK TO THE FUTURE

When you go **Back to the Future** you diverge to see, feel and touch the future vision you want to create. You are standing in the future and looking back to today. You then outline the steps you took to get there and achieve it. Relive how you harnessed your energy and bridged the gap from where you are today to where you were one year ago. Transport yourself forward to one year from today and write down the date. A reporter from a prestigious organization wants to write a feature article on what you accomplished over the past year. She is interested in how you were able to Take the Risk, Embrace Your Dream and take Proactive Actions to go get it. Use the questions that follow to stimulate your thinking for the article:

Future Vision Looking Back Questions

What *Dream* did you embrace? What *Shining Star* did you reach for?	What did you wish for and create? Why did you feel compelled to create it?
What makes this so unique and special?	Why is this so important to you?

What barriers did you have to overcome to realize this vision?	How wide was the gap between where you started one year ago to today?
What are associates, customers, family and friends saying about it? How are they reacting?	How does it feel to have achieved your vision, to have realized your *Dream?*
What words best describe what your success feels like and what is now happening?	Looking forward, where do you go from here?

Write your compelling story. Headline your article and use rich, vivid imagery. Draw out sharp contrasts between the future you've created, and the situation one short year ago. Have the reader feel the 'tension' that propelled your actions.

Headline:

Story:

With your compelling story in hand, propel forward and **Get the Facts**!

FIGHT THE RIGHT FOE

GET THE FACTS

Burst in here when…you have dared to dream and/or seen, felt, heard, and touched your future vision (from **Dare to Dream** and/or **Back to the Future**). Now it's time to discover and analyze the necessary data, details, facts and emotions to purposefully create tension and take the necessary action to close the gap between the current situation and the desired vision.

⒟IVERGENT WORKOUT

JUST THE FACTS PLEASE

When you get **Just the Facts Please** you diverge to discover and analyze the details, facts and opinions about your Dream/Big Goal Statements. Use the following questions to get a clearer picture of the data, details, facts and emotions required to make your vision a reality.

The Data, Details, Facts and Emotions Questions

What is a brief history of the situation?	What is the central challenge/ problem/opportunity?
What is the urgency, the seriousness of the issue?	What approaches have you tried previously, and what were the results?

What data, details, facts and opinions need to be discovered and analyzed?	What are the most pertinent facts?
Who else could offer a valuable perspective, and shed new light on the issues and data?	What is the impact if the problem goes unsolved or the opportunity isn't realized?
What are the root causes of the problems and/or performance issues?	What does the data not tell you?
What do your gut feelings, hunches and instincts tell you to do about this issue?	Given this information, what actions do you need to take to reach an ideal outcome for this situation?

Review the information that reveals new insights into the situation and is important to consider as you move forward. With your data, details, facts and emotions in hand, propel forward and **Clarify the Problem/Opportunity**.

FIGHT THE RIGHT FOE

CLARIFY THE PROBLEM/OPPORTUNITY

Burst in here when…you have discovered and analyzed the data, details, facts and emotions that are most pertinent to realizing your dream and achieving your desired vision. It's time to clarify, reframe and zero in on the specific problem/opportunity statements in order to transition and generate ideas to solve them.

⒟IVERGENT WORKOUT

REFRAME 'EM

When you **Reframe 'Em** you diverge and restate your problem/opportunity from differing perspectives (wide and narrow). Ideas follow how problems/opportunities are framed so it's good to be working from more, not less. Some statements will be more useful than others, but you can only assess that after you have worked with them. Use the statement starters: *'How to...' 'How might I...?' "In what ways might I...?'* Give the problem/opportunity pot a darn good stirring!

- Turn the data you identified previously into specific problem/opportunity statements.
- Take each barrier (what's stopping you from solving/pursuing it – real and/or perceived) and turn each one into a problem/opportunity statement.
- Think about how other people might frame the issue. For example, ask:

  - *"How would a highly skilled professional frame this issue?"*
  - *"How would a novice see it?"*
  - *"Who else had a similar challenge/problem/opportunity?"*
  - *"How might 007 or Wonder Woman approach this situation?"*
  - *"How could the problem/opportunity solve itself?"*
  - *"If you were working from a blank sheet of paper and weren't constrained by resources, how would you frame it?"*

- *"What are your assumptions about this issue?" "Which ones will need to be challenged?"*

Problem/Opportunity Statements

'How to...?' 'How might I...?' 'In what ways might I...?'

With your clarified problem/opportunity statements in hand, propel forward and **Evaluate and Select 'Em.**

©ONVERGENT WORKOUT

EVALUATE AND SELECT 'EM

When you **Evaluate and Select 'Em** you converge and prioritize the most feasible problem/opportunity statements you have generated. Use the following steps:

- Review the problem/opportunity statements you generated.
- Give each statement a letter, e.g., A, B, C, etc.
- With each statement ask, *"What do I think the impact will be when solved?"* Then ask, *"What do I think will be the degree of difficulty to solve it?"*

- Populate the letter on the matrix.
- If you have problem/opportunity statements with a high impact and high degree of difficulty to solve, generate ideas to reduce the difficulty.
- Hit the problem/opportunity statements to move forward with in order to generate ideas to solve.

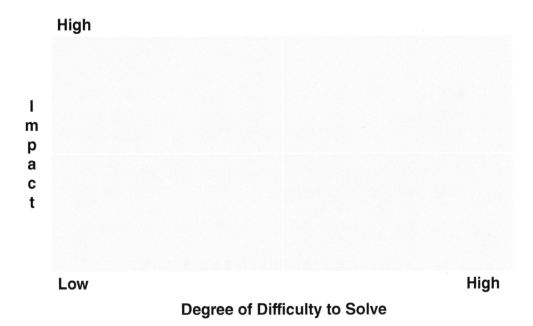

High

I m p a c t

Low   **High**

Degree of Difficulty to Solve

With your prioritized problem/opportunity statements in hand, you are ready to propel forward to **Episode ii, Imagination will Prevail: Battle #2**.

Summary of Episode i, Fight the Right Foe: Battle #1.

After priming the pump with many tips, tricks, tools, techniques and a comic strip to liberate your *B e y o n d e r Powers*, you burst in with your Dream/Big Goal, collaborated with *Black Diamond* and used your *Powers* of *Find It, See It* and *Be Versatile* to **Explore the Challenge, See the Future, Get the Facts** and **Clarify the Problem/Opportunity**. You *worked* out with **Dare to Dream, Back to the Future, Just the Facts Please, Reframe It** and **Evaluate and Select 'Em** and your outcome was clarified/prioritized Problem/Opportunity Statements. You have constructed a solid foundation to build on – *good energy*!

Glimpse forward to Episode ii, Imagination will Prevail: **Battles #2, #3 and #4:**

- **In Battle #2** Micro-Burst will Expose the True Colors of **Chameleon**. You will burst in with your Clarified/Prioritized Problem/Opportunity Statements, collaborate with *Micro-Burst* and use your *Powers* of *Be Fluent, Be Novel* and *Stay Open* to **Rain and Select Ideas**. Your outcome will be Hit Yes Ideas.

- **In Battle #3** Prism will Quiet **The Junk Yard Dog**. You will burst in with your Hit Yes Ideas, collaborate with *Prism*, and use your *Powers* of *Borrow It, Elaborate* and *Make New Connections* to **Take a Break and Incubate**. Your outcome will be More Hit Yes Ideas.

- **In Battle #4** Plusser will Strike Fear into **The 3 Headed Gremlin**. You will burst in with More Hit Yes Ideas, collaborate with *Plusser*, use your *Powers* of *Put Ideas in Context, Evaluate and Select It* and *Strengthen It* to **Strengthen the Concept**. Your outcome will be a Best Concept/Prototype.

MAKE A TWO-BOARD ADJUSTMENT

Reward Yourself

After you have successfully developed and implemented daily workouts and tests to strengthen your creativity, reward yourself. Money, chocolate and praise to name a few will work just fine.

EPISODE II
IMAGINATION WILL PREVAIL

PREVIEW

To ensure **Imagination will Prevail** *Micro-Burst, Prism* and *Plusser* prime the pump and fully unleash their sheer raw power of imagination. Their desired outcome is to generate *an abundance of novel, valuable and feasible ideas, cobble them together and strengthen them to be a* Best Concept /Prototype. To that end, there are three **Battles** in **Episode ii**:

- **Battle # 2**: *Micro-Burst* Exposes the True Colors of **Chameleon**
- **Battle # 3**: *Prism* Quiets **The Junk Yard Dog**
- **Battle # 4**: *Plusser* Strikes Fear into **The 3 Headed Gremlin**

However, **Chameleon, The Junk Yard Dog and The 3 Headed Gremlin** have different plans. They don't want to see any imagination—far from it. They aren't interested in attending the idea festival and didn't send back the RSVP. These burnt onion-smelling curmudgeons *kneel at the altar of conformity, habit, status-quo, predictability and fear!* They really like non-creative habits (checklists are their favorite), zero new stimulus, busyness, and more-of-the-same, retreaded non-imaginative ideas. From their very narrow way of thinking, imagination is for dreamers, pie in the skiers, people with their heads in the clouds and not grounded *in their pessimistic reality*. If you have any imagination left in you from childhood, don't worry, this merry band of **Resistors** will be more than happy to *stamp it out of you* once and for all! Ah yes, but they don't realize that storms are a-forming…three quite powerful idea storms that provide little or no warning are a-brewing.

One of nature's most dangerous storms is *a microburst*, a sudden downward burst of wind from the base of a thunderstorm. The air accelerates and crashes into the ground at 60 mph and spreads out in many directions. Winds at the surface can reach 100 mph. They tend to affect smaller areas, no larger than a few square miles. A *microburst* is a dangerous weather phenomenon that can cause great amounts of damage with little or no warning. We will pass on producing physical damage, but we do want to stir up some mighty strong wind gusts, get the currents flowing and ignite sudden bursts of novel and imaginative ideas with little or no warning. We want fast acceleration with ideas quickly spreading out in all directions. It takes big-time energy and possibility thinking to get things whipped up, and that's precisely what *Micro-Burst* intends to do.

But before we get hunting the good stuff **Chameleon** would very much appreciate it if we would obediently *adhere to the status-quo, conform to all social influences and pressures and just fit in for the rest of our lives thank you...*

JUST FITTING IN

No prison can hold me; no hand or leg irons or steel locks can shackle me. No ropes or chains can keep me from my freedom.

— Harry Houdini, Illusionist

In **What's Stopping You** we met the charming **Chameleon** as she was appropriately contrasted with her reptilian ancestors. To *chitch it* a bit, we transition to the sport of alpine skiing, because if she was a downhill skier she would always conform, fit in and stay on the well-groomed trails she knows, where she is supposed to be. She wouldn't ski too fast, and certainly

not veer off the groomed trails and ski the moguls—or heaven forbid, the fresh powder in the trees or in the back bowls. That would be too dangerous! Most certainly a safe skier, but one that would be a monumental bore to ski the backcountry with. When you consistently *stay on the well-groomed trails* you successfully exhibit status-quo thinking *being quite comfortable with and accepting of the current state-of-affairs as is.* The norm is to:

- Follow all culture, customs, rules and traditions.
- Stay on the well-groomed trails. Don't veer into someone else's trail or territory, or worse—get in their sandbox.
- Overemphasize the status-quo and more of the same thinking.
- Prematurely criticize ideas that break away from the way we do it and have always done it.
- Accept sub-optimal, cross-organizational collaboration.

CULTURE, CUSTOMS, RULES AND TRADITIONS THAT GUIDE PERSONAL, TEAM, ORGANIZATIONAL AND SOCIAL BEHAVIOR

Talent, I believe, is most likely to be found among nonconformists, dissenters and rebels.

— David Ogilvy, the father of advertising

Can **Culture, Customs, Rules and Traditions stifle novel thinking?** They sure can and they do. Every individual, family, team, social group, religion or organization can't function well without a baseline set of rules, laws, processes, hierarchy, culture, customs or traditions in place that serve as guides to govern accepted behavior. Without these, we would experience a level of confusion, chaos and possibly lawlessness that clearly wouldn't be acceptable. However, ask yourself: "*What are the results you get when you place subtle (and sometimes not-so-subtle) influences and pressures on people to fit in and conform, to acquiesce and accept restrictive pressures and to inhibit challenging the status-quo?*"

- We get our beloved compliance.
- We get people kneeling and saluting at the altar of conformity.
- Oh yes, we also get blessed with damn-close-to-zero imaginative thought.
- A few of my favorite (not) descriptions include: habit bound, conformity, turtle slow, inflexible, ritual, repressive, boring, territorial and angry.

When people overly adhere to the status-quo, they usually produce *more-of-the-same thinking and ideas*. This is rooted in a preference for what we know, staying in the safety of our current situation, not venturing out to vet alternative ideas and options we don't know yet. In the face of overpowering data, we sometimes choose the status-quo, the perceived safer choice, because we recognize and know it and aren't comfortable rocking the proverbial boat.

A *Beyonder* is *comfortable as a minority of one* (Torrance, 1999). People who are blessed with a direct dose have a fierce independent streak and are far less likely to bend their thinking and actions to social pressures. In the classic film *Gone with the Wind,* Clark Gable says to Vivian Leigh,

"Frankly my dear, I don't give a damn." Because *Beyonders* possess high levels of intrinsic task motivation and aren't influenced much by external evaluation and rewards (Amabile, 2012) they really don't give a damn what other people think.

I've had many people tell me they feel constrained because they have a top-heavy hierarchy to buck. They ask, *"Why stick my neck out, push against the hierarchy and take risks outside the safety of established and accepted norms and practices?"* This is a sane question. Certainly not advertised this way, the hierarchy typically defends the way things are done today. It employs Isaac Newton's Third Law of Motion: for every action (force) there is an equal and opposite reaction. This also plays out where ideas are judged prematurely, mistakes and failures are criticized. The hierarchy says it wants people to *fail fast*, but their actions don't always align with it. The prairies are dotted with graves of many bold non-conformers with arrows in their backs.

Unless the climate is supportive, it is uncomfortable to challenge the hierarchy when you see issues differently. More often than not it is far safer to not ask questions that challenge the *status-quo*. It's far more socially acceptable to be viewed as practical, logical and economical; to follow the rules and to not make waves. At a minimum we open ourselves up to elicit dissatisfaction, and at the outer limits can be criticized, ridiculed and even ostracized. Is it just me or have you also noticed that many highly creative people that don't fit in with the prevailing social orthodoxy or culture don't last all that long?

MAKE A TWO-BOARD ADJUSTMENT

Apply the Power of 3's

Practice the technique and then take a ten-minute break. Come back, practice the technique again, and take another ten-minute break. Then, conduct one additional round!

COULD WE TOP IF OFF WITH A LITTLE GROUPTHINK?

If we all think alike, no one is thinking.

— Benjamin Franklin, one of the Founding Fathers of the United States

In his classic book, *Victims of Groupthink: A Psychological Study of Foreign-Policy Decisions and Fiascoes*, social psychologist Irving Janis (1982) studied the theory of *groupthink*, defined as, *"a mode of thinking where individuals of a small cohesive group will acquiesce and accept a perceived group consensus viewpoint or conclusion, irrespective if they judge it to be valid, accurate or optimal."* His study centered on the impact of group-dynamic behaviors, biases, pressures and consensus-thinking on foreign-policy decisions, including the bombing of Pearl Harbor, the Vietnam War and the Bay of Pigs invasion. Janis examined why groups of smart people made bad decisions, identifying the following as symptoms of *groupthink*:

- Illusions of invulnerability, reading their own headlines, believing they are right and having an inability to accept being wrong.
- Rationalization of the group's decisions in the face of counter evidence. *"We've been right before when facing warnings to the contrary."*
- Complacency or even arrogance. With a track record of successful decisions, the presence of *'mindguards'* that shield or bias the group from alternative or negative information; overlooking potential consequences or risks downstream.
- Stereotyping key opponents and non-group members as not being up to the task. Not having the same firepower, not firing on as many cylinders as us.
- A loyalty pressure (e.g., being disloyal, fickle) placed on team members who raise an alternative or contrary opinion or viewpoint. Coupled with this is self-censorship: *"If I say something, I'll be viewed as disloyal or not as smart."*
- The illusion of decision unanimity among the group. Silence is not probed adequately and is interpreted as agreement.

Groupthink contributes to poor decision making; however, it isn't the sole contributor. There are a number of additional factors in play as well. On the plus side in specific contexts groupthink can accelerate decision making, and bolster the group's collective confidence in the decision. Following are three mechanisms to counterbalance groupthink:

1. Implement multiple communication channels for dissent to surface in decision making. Silence is not golden.
2. Empower people to *'stop the assembly line'* if they see a problem.
3. Encourage, incentivize and reward the surfacing of countervailing ideas.

GRIND THE GEARS

If left unchecked and unchallenged, these **Resistors** place unhealthy expectations and pressures that wreak havoc on our creative productivity. These influences impact our thinking by applying pressure on us to *conform to the way others expect us to think and behave*. The social pressure of conformity fuels the fear of being different and not fitting in. The result is a loss in our individuality and creative potential. If we don't force ourselves to challenge *more-of-the-same thinking,* we will continue to perpetuate the *status-quo.* History is replete with countless examples of this. When you grind the gears of status-quo thinking, you get innovation. Following are three gear grinders:

1. If Henry Ford emphasized the *status-quo* he would have found faster horses. Instead, he put his energy into mass producing automobiles.
2. If Dick Fosbury hadn't challenged *more-of-the-same thinking* in the high jump, he wouldn't have invented the Fosbury Flop, wouldn't have won the Olympic gold medal in 1968 and wouldn't have changed the high jump forever.
3. If Travis Kalanick and Garret Camp worried about *fitting in*, they wouldn't have identified and combined unmet transportation needs with a hot technology to create Uber and wouldn't have revolution-ized transportation services.

MAKE A TWO-BOARD ADJUSTMENT

Design a
Problem-Finding,
Idea-Seeking Work-Space

The workspace need not be fancy or sophisticated. In fact, it's preferable if it isn't. The key is to keep it visible, readily accessible and easy to use. A few ideas to *enhance your system*:

The purpose of the idea capture system is to record every idea, alternative or concept. The medium can be whatever you want that works. For example, use of post-it notes, a journal or notebook, markers, colored pencils, electronic devices: email, voicemail, iPhone, iPad, etc. My personal preference is to put one idea per post-it on an idea board and to organize them by themes.

The purpose of the visual display and communication system is to visually display the problems and ideas. The medium can be a whiteboard, wall posters, butcher paper, picture gallery shared collaboration workspaces, electronic blackboard, power point, etc. It is visible to all parties involved.

A place is to bring people together with 'stuff' readily available for prototyping, more diverging/converging (e.g., duct tape, magazines, catalogs) *to break set* and visually advance the sparkling ideas.

The purpose of the method is to manage the output weekly. Converge and select the best ideas with an eye to *get them to action*. Keep the process fresh and don't let the trail go cold. *Conversely, if you move too early*, you may act on inferior ideas because they were the first ones set out. Let the process unfold and work it every day. My dad used to ask me when he sensed inaction, "*Are you just going through the motions?*" It wasn't a question!

Speaking of **Not Fitting In**, I don't think we've been properly introduced…

...*MICRO-BURST*

was born to run and exemplifies that **Imagination will Prevail**. She has the unique *Power* to *Rain and Select Ideas*, an abundance of novel and feasible ones. Being a prolific rainmaker, she increases the likelihood of having an ample supply of novel ideas because she produces an abundance of them. She is cut from the cloth that more and novel is better—preferring to work from a large harvest of ideas and then whittle them down to the vital few.

Her *Powers* are:

Be Fluent

- Generate many ideas for open-ended problems and opportunities.
- Use wide and varied stimuli to jump-spark diverse thinking and ideas.
- Defer judgement when generating ideas, alternatives and concepts.
- Use mechanisms (e.g., quotas) to force generating an abundance of ideas.

Be Novel

- Resist conformity and be independent in thought and action.
- Seek originality, break away from obvious, habit-bound and automatic responses.
- Strive to generate exaggerated and wild ideas— the wilder the better.
- Break down the attributes/components of a problem or opportunity and generate ideas to improve each attribute/component.

Stay Open

- Take adequate time to fully understand the challenge, problem or opportunity and consider important factors about them.
- Think of ideas that are not merely extensions and more of the same.
- Keep ideas and options open for as long as possible and resist the strong knee-jerk temptation to prematurely reach conclusions.
- Seek out varied perspectives, points of view and opinions to gain an appreciative understanding of different or competing alternatives.

RAIN AND SELECT IDEAS

Disneyland will never be completed. It will continue to grow as long as there is imagination left in the world.

— Walt Disney, pioneer in the American animated film industry

ON THE EDGE

Whereas her adversary skis on the well-groomed trails, **Micro-Burst** does just the opposite and borrows the style of legendary downhill ski racer Franz Klammer of Austria. Nicknamed The Kaiser, many argue to this day that Klammer was the greatest downhill skier of all time. He won a staggering 26 World Cup races (12 in a row) and was a five-time World Cup champion. His average speed in the downhill in 1972 World Cup races was 111 mph, a record that stood for 25 years. He may be most widely known for his go-for-broke style in winning the gold medal in the downhill alpine race at the 1976 Winter Olympics in Innsbruck, Austria, recording a time of 1:45.73.

Klammer often skied on a razor-thin edge of control, bordering on calamity. In his own words he said, *"I knew I would win…I had to risk everything…It was me and the mountain…The crowd wanted me to win."* It was the greatest run the sport has ever witnessed (YouTube Videos: In Search of Speed, 2015). His goal was not to finish the race, nor to fit in with the other downhill skiers! Those thoughts never entered his mind. There was no room for them!

LESS IS NOT MORE

There is a long history in the creativity literature to support the premise that the more ideas a person generates *on the edge*, the higher the likelihood the ideas they develop will be robust and viable (Jung, 2015).

- This association between quantity and quality has been coined the 'equal-odds rule' (Simonton, 1997), which states, *"The relationship between the number of hits (creative successes) and the total number of works produced in a given time period is positive, linear and stable."*

- The degree to which the ideas generated are *on the edge*—truly novel and imaginative—further improve the odds that the concepts will gain real traction.

- Taking time to strengthen the best ideas to make them highly feasible further bolsters the chances that concepts will not only survive but will prosper.

Micro-Burst employs four *white hot* diverging principles to *get a-storming,* and four cooling converging principles to *get a-taming the wilder ones (if need be).*

GET A-STORMING DIVERGING PRINCIPLES (ADAPTED FROM OSBORN, 1993)

1. **Defer Judgment:** Possibly the cardinal principle and maybe the most difficult. We're well trained *not to defer judgment*, not to first identify what's right, or the potential of an idea when we or someone else proposes one. Heaven forbid we take time to list the plusses, potential and strengths of ideas, options and solutions. Instead, we often react to new approaches in the opposite way—first pointing out what's wrong with them. One of the reasons we often take an instant cool to new ideas (or dismiss them) is because they are outside our nine-dots frame of reference and experience. Just because we aren't familiar with them doesn't automatically make them wrong or inferior. The key skill is to separate diverging from converging. It's analogous to writing in that you can't write and edit well when you do them simultaneously. You have to put some time between the two thinking processes.

2. **Make Quantity Your Friend:** There is a correlation between the quantity of ideas and quality (Puccio, 2013). This principle may feel a bit counterintuitive because our natural inclination is to try to generate *good quality ideas*. The mind only starts getting juiced once the obvious ideas are generated. You have a much higher likelihood of coming up with a really good idea if you are working from many. Said differently, if you only have one really good idea *you are in a heap of trouble!* Give yourself a quota of at least two baker's-dozen ideas or alternatives that might possibly solve your challenge, problem or opportunity. Even as you see good ideas emerge, keep pushing for more quantity.

3. **Seek Wild and Unusual Ideas:** The wilder and more unusual the better. It's more exhilarating to try to tame a wild mustang than to try to make a plow horse gallop. Go beyond the obvious and strive for novelty. In his bestselling book, *A Whack on the Side of the Head*, Roger Van Och [1998] introduced stepping stones, like those in a stream, hopping from one stone to another to potentially lead to a novel concept. At times we may have to back off a really big idea, but we can use pieces or parts of it to spur additional thought (i.e., *while we can't do that, we could do this…*). Stepping-stones help us step or jump to the novelty. Here's a high-bar test for novelty: Come up with an idea so outrageous that when you present it to your boss you are guaranteed to be fired on the spot, no doubt about it! We're now making real novelty progress.

4. **Build on, Combine, Hitchhike and Synthesize Ideas:** By applying the first three principles you will have produced a bounty of high-quality, fresh ingredients and spices, and now it's time to combine them into a unique dish. Yes, experiment with and force many new idea combinations, alternatives and options. I'm looking for *the next right idea, the next right idea combination*. The majority of new ideas are new combinations. What's new is the combination—the way it's put together. Case in point: Ben & Jerry's line up of ice cream has lots of interesting flavor combinations, names and images.

TAME 'EM CONVERGING PRINCIPLES (ADAPTED FROM OSBORN, 1993)

1. **Be Affirmative:** While converging, it's important to stay open to potentials. Stay positive, open and affirm novelty! New or seemingly opposing ideas may help sharpen your thinking or spark new ideas.

2. **Be Deliberate:** Give ideas a fair hearing. Avoid snap, knee-jerk judgments and premature decisions. Recognize, call out and manage your preconceived assumptions and biases. Similar to deferring judgment, keep ideas open for as long as you possibly can to avoid the strong temptation to prematurely decide.

3. **Align Ideas with your Objectives:** Ensure the ideas generated support and align with your objectives. Don't get sidetracked with cool ideas that aren't tracking and connected with your objectives.

4. **Stay Open to Novelty:** Encourage novelty to flow even as you work to winnow down the number of ideas. If the hot blue sparks are a-flying, fan 'em. If need be, modify your selection criteria. Don't squeeze original thinking.

LESSONS FROM THE RENAISSANCE

In a comprehensive study on the history of creativity, Dr. Keith Simonton (1981) from the University of California reported the highest levels of creative output occurred in times and places marked with wide levels of cultural diversity and intense political upheaval. In ancient Greece from where many of the great philosophers emanated, there were fierce rivalries between the city-states of Athens, Corinth, Sparta and others. In Renaissance Italy, rivalries between the city-states of Venice, Milan, Florence, Naples and Genoa sparked unprecedented levels of creativity. Great artisans such as Leonardo da Vinci, Michelangelo, Dante and a host of others emerged and prospered during that era. The region was a true hotbed of talent. Simonton argues that greater levels of creativity flourished throughout history when there were clashes between rival states. He reported a time lag of about twenty years before the creativity flourished—after parents instilled it in their children, and when they came of age. An especially turbulent time took place in Europe from the 14th to 17th century, one of the most creative times in history. Turbulence sparks creativity.

Chameleon is a sworn enemy of environments where people are encouraged *to challenge* barriers that inhibit novel thinking and to question inflexible rules, traditions and customs. She doesn't see the need for '*rock throwers*' who challenge overly restrictive rules, traditions and methods and ask healthy questions like:

Why do we do it this way?	Says who?	Who said this can't be changed?
Where is this written in stone?	Isn't it better to ask for forgiveness than to ask for permission?	Who says it's solely the job of marketing and product management to identify the needs of customers?

These kinds of questions are unnerving to bureaucracies. If you want more innovation, more challenging questions need to be asked *more frequently*. You want a climate where people can freely go up to the edge, look down into the canyon and think about *R E V O L T*—in a 'quasi' respectful and lawful manner of course. Innovation demands more independent thought because without it, the **hot blue sparks** won't get flying fast or hot enough. So, just for s…s and giggles, what if we emphasize and practice challenging most everything that restricts independent and creative thought, quasi respectfully of course.

BEYOND THE BOUNDARIES

Perfection is not attainable, but if we chase perfection,
we can catch excellence.

— Vince Lombardi, legendary NFL coach of the Green Bay Packers

Novel, spicy ideas are most often found beyond the edges, at the extremes, at the exaggerations. You have to fall in every once in a while to know just how close you are to the edge. In fact, you may very well have to fall in frequently. When you exaggerate ideas, you push them beyond existing parameters and current constraints. You can exaggerate by asking the following: "*How to perfectly solve this problem? What ideas could make this situation perfect? How could the problem solve itself?*" The concept of perfect is an exaggeration. It's at the extreme, beyond the edges. Make it a habit to use exaggerations!

MAKE A TWO-BOARD ADJUSTMENT

Conduct Smart Repetitions

Start with a small number of repetitions to train your technique. Add more over time, make the repetitions smart, and don't go through the motions. With smart repetitions, a training habit will begin to feel more natural. With smart repetitions, the goal is to perfect the technique! Let me repeat that—to perfect the technique. Experimenting is a spring board to strengthen skills. The outcome is muscle memory where you don't have to think about it; it has become automatic and is anchored as a repeatable, everyday habit.

Better batten down the hatches, brace for the fast-approaching storm, and get a front-row seat to watch *The B e y o n d e r* who can really get the *hot blue flames and sparks* a-sparking and a-flying when…

BATTLE #2
MICRO-BURST
EXPOSES THE TRUE COLORS
OF CHAMELEON

Her *Powers* are:

- *Be Fluent*
- *Be Novel*
- *Stay Open*

Rules, Traditions & Cultural Resistorss

- An Overemphasis of the Status-Quo
- Social Influences and Conformity Pressures

ASSUMPTIONS ARE SO EMBEDDED INTO OUR WAY OF THINKING THAT WE DON'T EVEN NOTICE THEM.

YOU KNOW WHAT YOU DO WHEN YOU *ASSUME*, DON'T YOU? YOU MAKE AN A...

LET THE LADY TALK!

FIRST IDENTIFY YOUR ASSUMPTIONS...

HOW TO REDUCE CYCLE TIME IN HIRING PROSPECTIVE EMPLOYEES AND HIRE PEOPLE WHO ARE EXCEPTIONAL CREATIVE-PROBLEM-SOLVERS?

THERE HAS TO BE FORMAL INTERVIEWS.
IT HAS TO BE PANEL INTERVIEWS.
MUST BE CONDUCTED IN TRADITIONAL SETTING.
LED BY THE COMPANY HIRING MANAGER.
GOTTA HAVE TRADITIONAL RESUME.

THEN PHRASE THEM IN **REVERSE**.

THIS CHALLENGES THE STATUS QUO AND GENERATES NEW PERSPECTIVES FOR PROBLEM SOLVING!

NO INTERVIEWS?

TRAINING AS INTERVIEW?

INTERVIEWEE LEADS INTERVIEW?

- RE-WRITE RESUME WITH INTERVIEWERS?

- COFFEE SHOP CHAT INTERVIEW?

- SWEEPSTAKES CONTESTS

(E.G. MOST COMPELLING RESUME)

EPISODE PROFILE:
DICK FOSBURY

I adapted an antiquated style and modernized it into something that was efficient. I didn't know anyone else in the world would be able to use it, and I never imagined it would revolutionize the event.

— Dick Fosbury, Olympic champion and inventor of the Fosbury Flop

THE FOSBURY FLOP

Merriam-Webster defines *iconoclast* as *a person who criticizes or opposes beliefs and practices that are widely accepted.* Dick Fosbury of the United States won the gold medal and set an Olympic record in the high jump—jumping 2.24 meters (7.35 feet) at the Summer Olympics in Mexico City, Mexico on October 20, 1968. It marked the international debut of his jumping style, *The Fosbury Flop.*

Prior to *The Flop,* athletes either approached the bar straight on or approached it diagonally and threw both legs over the bar in a scissor motion. Athletes improved the scissor method with a straddle technique where they approached the bar at a diagonal angle, used their inner leg to take off and then thrust the outer leg up to lead the body sideways over the bar. To land safely, athletes had to jump carefully because the landing pits consisted only of sawdust and lower matting. In the 1960s, the landing pits were upgraded using softer and raised landing mats. Fosbury recognized the importance of this upgrade and it sparked the idea for him to experiment with a new jumping method.

Rather than using the traditional scissors or straddle style forward kick over the bar, Fosbury used a mid-air rotation so he could land on the mat with the back of his head. He explained that by taking off on his right or outside foot he could turn his back to the bar and kick his legs out to clear the bar. Fosbury explained:

"The advantage of the technique from a physics perspective is it allows you to run at the bar with greater speed and with an arch in your back. You could clear the bar and maintain your center of gravity at or below the bar, making it much more efficient."

At the time it looked odd, but it worked better than the other techniques. One journalist described the technique *"looking like a guy falling off the back of a truck."* Another said, *"he looked like a fish flopping in a boat."* U.S. Olympic Coach Pat Jordan predicted *"it could wipe out a generation of high jumpers, they will suffer broken necks."*

Source, International Olympic Committee

They were all wrong. Fosbury had invented a new technique and revolutionized the sport. By 1980, the majority of the world's elite high jumpers, and almost every gold medal winner and major record holder was using *The Flop.*

Pay Attention. Your Environment may be Changing Right Before your Eyes: The sport of high jumping changed in the 1960's because of the upgrade to landing pits, enabling athletes to experiment with a broader range of techniques. Most athletes didn't recognize this shift and continued to use the same techniques and jumped the same way. That of course was until Dick Fosbury came on the scene, paid attention and revolutionized the sport...with *The Flop*!

A Provocative Question: What dynamics are changing in your environment right now that provide an opportunity for you to be fearless, to be an iconoclast and to revolutionize your sport?

IT'S YOUR TIME

In the comic strip *Micro-Burst* used her *Powers* of *Be Fluent, Be Novel* and *Stay Open* to Expose the True Colors of **Chameleon** and help the recruiting team **Rain and Select Ideas** to solve their prioritized problems/opportunities. She boldly proclaims that **Imagination will Prevail!**

It's Your Time to continue the journey, prime the pump, jump spark your energy and powerhouse. *Work out* with **Reverse the Hidden Assumptions** and **Hit 'Em** and accelerate your velocity to *Lean into Risk, Embrace Your Dream and Take Proactive Actions to go get it!*

EPISODE II, RAIN AND SELECT IDEAS! BATTLE #2

BURST IN HERE WHEN...

You have clarified/ prioritized problem/ opportunity statements, and need to **Rain and Select** novel and feasble ideas to solve them.

AND FIGHT OFF CHAMELEON AND HER RULES, TRADITIONS AND CULTURAL RESISTORS:

- An Overemphasis of the Status-Quo
- Social Influences and Conformity Pressures

POWER SOURCES

- Clarified/ Prioritized Problem/ Opportunity Statements

...MICRO-BURST

CHAMELEON

 **VS.**

POWERS

- Be Fluent
- Be Novel
- Stay Open

KEY ACTIONS

- Rain and Select Ideas

WORKOUTS

- Reverse the Hidden Assumptions
- Hit 'Em

OUTCOMES

HIT YES IDEAS!

IMAGINATION WILL PREVAIL

RAIN AND SELECT IDEAS

Burst in here when...you have clarified and prioritized your problem/opportunity statements and want to **Rain and Select** an abundance of novel and feasible ideas to solve them.

(D)IVERGENT WORKOUT

REVERSE THE HIDDEN ASSUMPTIONS

When you **Reverse the Hidden Assumptions**, you diverge and reverse it, look at things in contrarian ways, combat oppressive conformity and social pressures. You shake it up, exaggerate and distort it. You think wishfully and escape from what you take for granted. You expose and challenge the underlying assumptions about the problem or opportunity. Taking these actions will enable you to examine the conditions and assumptions you may take for granted. From there, break your fixed thinking, perceiving and responding patterns and examine what would happen if you reversed your set of assumptions.

Bring forward your clarified/prioritized problem/opportunity statements from **Fight the Right Foe** and populate them in the following chart:

Problem/Opportunity Statements

'How to...?'	'How might I...?'	'In what ways might I...?'

Put on your rain gear and get **Raining Ideas**. Remember to:

- Defer judgment
- Generate quantity
- Seek wild and unusual ones—the wilder the better
- Build on, combine, hitchhike, piggyback and synthesize ideas

Use the following steps to **Reverse the Hidden Assumptions**:

- Identify your assumptions about the problem/opportunity and populate those in the Assumptions Column.
- Reverse each of the assumptions. Ask: *'What is the opposite of each assumption?'* Populate the reversed assumptions in the Reversed Assumptions Column.
- With each reversed assumption, ask: *'How can I use this reversed assumption?'* *'What ideas does it spark for me?'* Populate these ideas in the Novel, Spicy Ideas Column.

Novel, Spicy Idea Rack

Assumptions	Reversed Assumptions	Novel, Spicy Ideas

You **Rained** a bountiful quantity of novel, spicy ideas to solve the problem/opportunity. Now, move forward, converge and **Hit 'Em.**

ⓒONVERGENT WORKOUT

HIT 'EM

When you **Hit 'Em** you converge and select the most feasible idea options. Use the following steps:

- With the Decision Selection Grid, identify the criteria to use to judge your idea options and list them across the top row labeled Criteria. Make sure the criteria is as specific as possible.
- List the ideas in the column directly below Idea Options.
- Working with one idea at a time and moving from left to right, judge if the idea option meets each of the criteria. If a yes **Hit 'Em** and check the box. If a no, leave it blank. Follow the same process for each idea option.
- If warranted, generate ways to strengthen the idea options that don't successfully meet the criteria.
- Once completed, review the grid to get a visual representation of your selections. The ideas with the most checks are your best Hit Yes Ideas to move forward with.

Decision Selection Grid

Criteria Idea Options						

Summary of Episode ii, Imagination will Prevail, Battle #2: Micro-Burst Exposes the True Colors of Chameleon

After priming the pump with many tips, tricks, tools, techniques and a comic strip to liberate your *B e y o n d e r Powers*, you burst in with your Clarified/Prioritized Problem/Opportunity Statements, collaborated with *Micro-Burst* and used your *Powers* of *Be Fluent, Be Novel* and *Stay Open* to **Rain and Select Ideas**. You *worked out* with **Reverse the Hidden Assumptions** and **Hit 'Em** and your outcome was Hit Yes Ideas. Good work, you significantly increased the likelihood of success. Onward, it's time to collaborate with *Prism*!

Glimpse forward to Episode ii, Imagination will Prevail, Battle #3: Prism Quiets The Junk Yard Dog.

You will burst in with your Hit Yes Ideas, collaborate with *Prism*, use your *Powers* of *Borrow It, Elaborate* and *Make New Connections* to **Take a Break and Incubate** and produce even More Hit Yes Ideas. You will soon be working from the power of abundance, reinforcing that less is not more!

COWS DRINK MILK

THINKING, PERCEIVING AND RESPONDING IN HABIT-BOUND WAYS

You're only given a little spark of madness. You mustn't lose it.

— Robin Williams, comedian and actor

The Junk Yard Dog barks at everything, anything and everybody he isn't familiar with, doesn't recognize, doesn't know and isn't his habit. He isn't the least bit interested and doesn't want to become familiar with any deviation from **Thinking, Perceiving and Responding in Habit-Bound Ways.**

Hitting the comfortable habit and learning button and going in a time-efficient way through our daily routines is a necessary, adaptive survival skill. It would be virtually impossible to get through most days without doing so. Being a creature of habit is certainly a plus for getting us through our hectic schedules. However, it is also *a big smelly old fat onion* that blocks our creative potential.

Most of us learned early in life there were *correct* and *incorrect* ways of thinking, perceiving and responding to issues and situations. There was a clear, identifiable path to the more acceptable responses, routines and patterns of behavior. We learned the way things were done, and how they were expected to be done. We learned how and where to categorize ideas. As we have made our way through life, it can be quite difficult to break from these *original truths, routines and habits* and create something that is truly unique and differentiated.

Thinking, Perceiving and Responding Resistors find their roots in how we learn and the habits we formed. We become comfortable and accustomed to collecting, organizing, evaluating and understanding data, problems, ideas, issues and people in familiar and predictable ways. Consequently, we experience **very little variance, almost zero**. In craving predictability, we unwittingly place mental blocks in our way that make it more difficult to see or explore new questions, ideas, alternatives, possibilities, uses or applications. *When was the last time you truly created or experienced something dramatically new and exciting? Are your customary ways and habits of thinking, perceiving and responding* *getting you the results you want? Are your expectations getting in the way of finding and framing new problems and raining ideas that aren't simply more of the same?* Yes, **The Junk Yard Dog** enjoys nothing more than a very dry oasis, having virtually *0 Variance in his routine.* His pet phrase is, *"The habit made me do it."*

Social psychologists define this rigidity of thinking, perceiving and responding as *cognitive, functional, or perceptual fixedness* (Amabile, 1996, Ramos, 2017). Why is it so difficult to break habits, think, perceive and respond to things in new lights? The following three points shed light on this cool, calculating **Resistor**:

- We learn and are programmed to repeat success patterns and not to proactively look for new patterns. It's at the core of evolution and biological reproduction. We perceive that most existing ideas are good because they are familiar, within our nine dots frame of reference. As a result, we set the trap for ourselves that many new ideas are *wrong* because they break from our success patterns, our nine dots, the way we know how to do things and make them work.

- Consciously breaking from the past is contrary to being efficient and getting our work done. It is more efficient to repeat what we know. With *everyday work* the goal is zero variance. We want to repeat tasks the same way every time. We want a zero failure rate. For good reason we want our surgeons and pilots to perform their tasks the best way they know how, every time, no exceptions (note: everyday work and creative work is explained in more detail in **Episode iii: Extreme Time Pressures**)!

- Perceptual fixedness is rooted in our inclination to leap to conclusions, make quick decisions without first evaluating other options. This tendency prevents us from assessing the situation and getting a more complete picture of what is happening. If we diagnose a problem based on familiar symptoms or continue to use the same techniques and don't challenge them, we may *treat the wrong problem or not recognize a more effective technique.* Many an auto mechanic, teacher and physician unfortunately fall prey to these tendencies.

In my workshops I conduct a *'cows drink milk'* exercise by pointing to the flipchart paper and asking, *"What color is this?"* Most people answer *white.* I ask them to shout it out and they shout out *white,* with each response being louder. I then ask, *"What do cows drink?"* Most people answer *milk.* I ask them to shout it out and they shout *milk.* I pause and ask, *"What do cows drink?"* Most people then answer *water.* This exercise illustrates perceptual conditioning where the words white, cows and milk seem to go together. The perception is fixed until we challenge our thinking. In this case the perception is incorrect. Our perceiving can become quite automatic, quite Pavlovian don't you think?

We all have degrees of cognitive, functional or perceptual fixedness based on our history, experiences, interests and needs. The challenge is to view *'old things'* through a new prism to see new applications, uses and ways. Walt Disney didn't invent theme parks—he saw something different and made old theme parks brand new. What do you say we invite in **The B e y o n d e r** that can give the pot a real good stirring, get it a-shaking and a-baking with some new, hot, spicy idea combinations?

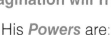...*PRISM*

has a keen instinct and knows when to **Take a Break and Incubate** on ideas; generate additional ones, and cobble together a spicy new mix of idea combinations. He knows that ideas flow in many directions: they can be expanded, contracted and combined. In developing new idea combinations and integrating ideas from his **sidekick** *Micro-Burst*, he is a true believer and living proof that **Imagination will Triumph.**

His *Powers* are:

Borrow It

- Think analogically, borrow ideas from one context and apply them in another.
- See a connection from a related problem or idea and repurpose it.
- Look laterally for ideas in suitable applications or industries.
- Discover how nature goes about solving similar issues.

Elaborate

- Expound on ideas by adding enough detail to them, but not excessively.
- Develop ideas by improving, embellishing or transforming them.
- Frame ideas so they can be understood by other people and aren't perceived to be too complex, costly or far out.
- Orchestrate the details of ideas so it is clear what actions should be taken by whom, by when and with what resources.

Make New Combinations

- Modify attributes and components of ideas into new configurations.
- Challenge the underlying assumptions of a problem or opportunity and reverse them to develop new combinations.
- Take something that currently exists and adapt it to develop new applications, purposes, relationships or uses.
- Combine and force-connect things together that on the surface appear to be incongruent and not fit together.

TAKE A BREAK AND INCUBATE

THE IMPORTANCE OF ANALOGICAL THINKING

Good writers borrow ideas; great writers steal them.

— T.S. Eliot, poet, publisher, playwright and literary critic

Being a student of physics, **Prism** knows that when light passes through a prism and is refracted by the angles and plane faces of the prism, each wavelength of light is refracted by a different amount. Red has the lowest frequency and is refracted the least; violet has the highest frequency and is refracted the most. Not bothered by a barking **Junkyard Dog**, he experiments with many new idea combinations by reframing and refracting them—wide, beyond current boundaries and narrow, in between the lines.

All creative thinking skills are important. However, it's hard to overstate the importance of *analogical thinking*. A number of creativity researchers (Davis, 2004; Sterrnberg, 1999; Torrance, 1999) among others, support the premise that many of our most creative ideas have their roots in analogical thinking. When we think analogically, *we borrow ideas* from one situation or context and *force-connect them* to a different situation or context, producing new ideas and idea combinations in the process. And no, the bird of paradise will not fly on by and plop new ideas from the sky onto our laps. New ideas don't appear out of thin air, they originate from somewhere. Following are six examples that underscore the vital importance of analogical thinking:

- Bill Klann of the Ford Motor Company got the idea to speed up production of the Model T after visiting the Swift Company's slaughterhouse in Chicago where he saw butchers performing specialized tasks, cutting up carcasses as they moved along overhead trolleys. Klann borrowed the idea to design a moving assembly line with auto workers performing specialized tasks.

- Swiss engineer and amateur mountaineer George de Mestral went hiking in the woods with his dog and upon returning home took note of the burrs that clung to his clothes. He wondered if this sticking idea could be useful in commercial application. This connection led to the invention of Velcro.

- The idea for Pringles potato chips was sparked by the analogy of wet leaves which stack compactly and do not destroy themselves.

- Steve Jobs of Apple was exposed to the computer mouse and graphical user interface (click, virtual buttons) at Xerox's Palo Alto Research Center. He used this insight coupled with other hardware and software advances to make personal computers accessible, easy to use and affordable.

- Eiji Kakatsu, GM of technical development for the bullet trains of Japan, was confronted with severe noise problems from early designs. Upon listening to a lecture on birds from an aviation engineer, he led a design team to model the nose of the train after the beak of the Kingfisher bird because they have specialized beaks that allow them to dive into water at high speeds to hunt with a minimal splash.

- Architect Mick Pearce and engineers from the company Arup designed the ventilation system for the Eastgate Centre in Harare, Zimbabwe. With no conventional air conditioning or heating system it stays regulated year round with dramatically less energy consumption. The design methods were inspired from indigenous Zimbabwean masonry and the self-cooling mounds of African termites. Termites keep their gigantic mounds at exactly 87 degrees F (so they can farm a fungus that is their primary food source), while the temperatures outside range from 35 degrees F at night to 104 degrees F during the day. The termites achieve this by consistently opening and closing a series of heating and cooling vents throughout the mound during the day. With adjusted convection currents, air is sucked in at the base of the mound, down into enclosures with muddy walls, and up through a channel to the peak of the mound.

TUNE IN

Passion is energy. Feel the power that comes from what excites you.

— Oprah Winfrey, media executive and philanthropist

Speaking of analogical thinking, how about tuning in to what is occurring in front of you right now? Stop the action and observe, question and examine what is present before you. Wake up, reinvigorate your curiosity and rediscover your sense of wonder, your ability to be awed! Pioneers, scientists, artists, musicians and entrepreneurs among others have a unique capacity, a willingness to value the power of insightful questions. Smart answers follow insightful questions. American philosopher and educator John Dewey (Dworkin, 1959) reminds us that, *"A problem well-defined is half solved."*

In his book, *Everyday Wonders*, Barry Evans (1993) takes us on journeys to commonplace concepts such as gravity, water, our eyes' sensitivity to color, and *tunes the reader into* delightful adventures to see again what has always been there, waiting to be rediscovered. See things without preconditions as if seeing them for the first time. See them like an amateur, a child, and not a seasoned cowboy/cowgirl of oh so many rodeos. When we *tune in* we see new alternatives, ideas and combinations *beyond often self-imposed boundaries*! New combinations trigger new ideas (e.g., chocolate and peanut butter, home shopping network, the iPhone, etc.). Take the time to fully leverage your knowledge and experience and combine it with discovery and observation skills to think about and perceive the environment and surroundings. I suspect one of the main culprits that gets in the way are the constant demands of everyday life: the commute, the meetings, the pressure for short-term results, the kids, the conflicts and the money demands. How about making daily appointments with yourself (and keeping them) and take the time to pay attention, *tune in* and re-spark your sense of wonder?

SHAKE, BAKE AND INCUBATE

The *process of incubation* is a bit mysterious because it involves our conscious and subconscious thinking and our ability to process information. As such we can't see it, hear it or put our hands on it. It's not typically viewed as *a 'deliberate step'* in creative thinking, but one that occurs after we pause in our conscious and deliberate effort to solve something. We step away from the issue, put some distance between it and sleep on it!

The mental process of incubation may best be understood by linking it to **Micro-Burst**'s *Get-a-Storming Diverging Principle, Defer Judgment*. When we defer judgment and don't force a decision prematurely, we enable problems, sub-problems, ideas and actions to flow freely to our associative thinking processes. Our minds are quite capable of thinking about past experiences, and in a parallel action think about things in our present awareness and naturally link and integrate them. When we only consciously search for pairings, links or connections can be missed. The unconscious mind is very capable of attending to a good amount of activity whereas the conscious mind is more limited to the number of issues it can focus on at one time (Parnes, 1992). No precise formula exists for how long we should allow our questions and ideas to incubate and marinate (darn), however food sure tastes better when it has first been marinated. In **Episode iii** we will further explore *active intuition*, ways to prime and accelerate it. Passive intuition, waiting for the idea to hit is a little like sitting around and watching paint dry—boring! But for now, a key takeaway is to deliberately integrate more incubation time periods into your problem solving, idea finding efforts. Take advantage of the natural power of incubation to work and allow insights, ideas and new combinations to find you. More novel ideas jump into an optimistic and calm mind!

JUMP SPARK NOVEL IDEAS

If I see anything vital around me, it is precisely that spirit of adventure which seems indestructible and is akin to curiosity.

— Maire Curie, the first woman to be awarded the Nobel Prize (twice)

Transitioning from the preceding tranquil section, can we pick up the pace now people and get fanning more **hot blue flames** to get the sparks a flying in this kitchen? Where is the shake and bake? We need a short order idea cook, slinging the new idea combination hash, and a lot of it!

Incubation doesn't infer idleness. We can simultaneously step away from a problem at hand/the ideas we've generated *and* put ourselves in a place of most potential. Namely, *jump spark* various ways to frame the problem or opportunity, and then generate additional questions, ideas and concepts. Combine the practices of incubation, analogical thinking and *taking an excursion or two*. Put that trio into a cocktail shaker and give it a good shake. Just for the heck of it, add to the mix a spicy idea checklist. To borrow from the wonderful musical film, *Mary Poppins*, here are a few of my favorite things…and *idea-sparking questions*:

- How does nature solve it? What if we exaggerated it? What if we made it perfect? How about a blend? What else is like this? Who has already solved this? Who could be copied? How to take value and blow the top off it? How to increase value inexpensively? What if we changed colors, taste, visuals, sounds or feel? What if we made it stronger? How about adding in a secret sauce ingredient or two? How to minimize it? How to adapt it for many other uses? What new ways to use as-is? What new applications to use as-is? What to do without? How to change the pace? How to change the schedule, the timing? How about doing the opposite? What if we turn it backward? Just suppose we reverse roles?

MAKE A TWO-BOARD ADJUSTMENT

Integrate Excursions into your Weekly Routines

Excursions are techniques that help us break our thinking and perceiving patterns. *The objective is to immerse yourself early and often in the places of most potential.* Don't look in places just because the light is on there. Bring your lantern or helmet light and look in the most opportune places. While there are many ways to take an *Excursion*, following are three good ones:

Conduct literature scans of diverse materials to include trend data, publications, magazines, newspapers, websites, videos and books. Look for ideas in unique places and ask how you can apply these ideas to your challenge, problem or opportunity.

Go on a wide variety of diverse physical field visits: conduct interviews, observe, walk the processes where you want to gain keen insight.

Develop, nurture and diversify your idea generation network to include learning events, shows, conferences and networking events. Ask: Which outside experts to tap into? What outsiders to bring in? What other networks or groups of people to get integrated into? Consider factors such as diverse cultures, countries or origin, gender, age, political and socio-economic status, professional occupations, levels within organizations and industries.

And speaking of generating new, dynamic idea combinations for crying out loud, can you keep it down out there? We're trying to think in here as **Prism gets ready to quiet The Junk Yard Dog!**…

BATTLE #3

...PRISM
QUIETS
THE JUNK YARD DOG

His *Powers* are:

- *Borrow It*
- *Elaborate*
- *Make New Connections*

Thinking and Perceiving Resistors

- **Thinking, Perceiving and Responding in Habit-Bound Ways.**

PRISM QUIETS THE JUNKYARD DOG

PETE'S IS A SMALL 3RD GENERATION FAMILY OWNED RESTAURANT FEATUR-ING HOMEMADE ITALIAN AND IRISH FOODS NESTLED IN A SMALL CITY IN THE CENTER OF A ONCE BUSTLING PAPER MILL FACTORY DISTRICT ALONGSIDE THE RAGING BLACK RIVER.

ONLY ONE MILL REMAINS OPEN IN TOWN. MANY HOME OWNERS HAVE MOVED TO THE "OTHER SIDE OF THE TRACKS" AND THE YOUNGER GENER-ATION IS LOOKING FOR A DIFFERENT DINING EXPERIENCE.

UNFORTUNATELY, THE GOLDEN DAYS OF THE PAPER MILL INDUSTRY ARE LONG IN THE REAR VIEW MIRROR, EMPLOYMENT AT THE MILLS HAS PLUMMETED AND CONSEQUENTLY BUSINESS IN THE RESTAURANT HAS SUFFERED.

HOWEVER, TOURISM HAS PICKED UP AS THREE ADVENTURE COMPANIES HAVE OPENED WHERE THE MIGHTY BLACK RIVER RUNS FAST AND BEGUN OFFERING SEASONAL WHITEWATER RIVER RAFTING TRIPS TO THE BRAVE AT HEART.

THROUGH THE YEARS, PETE'S CATERED TO WALK IN CUSTOMERS.

THEY COME FOR THE AFFORD-ABLE FOOD AND DRINK, JOYOUS ATMOSPHERE AND FELLOWSHIP.

PETE AND MARY CALL A FAMILY MEETING TO DISCUSS IDEAS TO REVERSE THE SLIDE IN SALES.

WE THINK WE SHOULD DOUBLE DOWN AND KEEP DOING WHAT MADE US SUCCESSFUL IN THE FIRST PLACE. REPEAT THE FORMULA –

POSSIBLY EXPAND THE MENU AND ADVERTISE ON THE BACK PAGE OF THE LOCAL NEWSPAPER THE WAY WE HAVE ALWAYS DONE IT. LET'S JUST DO MORE OF IT.

EPISODE PROFILE:
THOMAS EDISON

Our greatest weakness lies in giving up.
The most certain way to succeed is always to try just one more time.

— Thomas Edison, American Inventor

Source, Google Images

Thomas Alva Edison is recognized by many historians as America's greatest inventor. At the time of his death in 1931 Edison held 1,093 U.S. patents. He executed his first patent application in October, 1868 at the age of 21. He also filed an estimated 600 unsuccessful or abandoned patent applications. He pioneered a model for modern industrial research.

Edison is famous for commercializing the incandescent light bulb, developing the phonograph and the motion picture camera. And while these inventions were built from many experiments, one that isn't as celebrated is his work to develop the alkaline storage battery. Edison ran over a reported 10,000 experiments with different materials and chemicals to develop the alkaline storage battery. In *His Life and Inventions,* Frank Dyer *(2010 ed.)* captures the Herculean efforts from Edison's friend and associate, Walter S. Mallory:

"This [the research] had been going on more than five months, seven days a week, when I was called down to the laboratory to see him [Edison]. I found him at a bench about three feet wide and twelve feet long, on which there were hundreds of little test cells that had been made up by his corps of chemists and experimenters. I then learned that he had thus made over nine thousand experiments in trying to devise this new type of storage battery but had not produced a single thing that promised to solve the question. In view of this immense amount of thought and labor, my sympathy got the better of my judgment, and I said: '*Isn't it a shame that with the tremendous amount of work you have done you haven't been able to get any results?'* Edison turned on me like a flash, and with a smile replied: *'Results! Why, man, I have gotten lots of results! I know several thousand things that won't work!'*

Many ideas start off as a hunch, an instinct, a feeling, a spontaneous thought. How about you **run an experiment and test it**? Experiment and test it early and do it as inexpensively as possible. The cost of early experimenting and testing is quite low in comparison with those further downstream. Learn from the experiments and tests, make adjustments and move forward. Take your sparks of novel ideas—test them, learn from them, make adjustments, and act on them. What three parallel experiments can you run right now to test your hunches, your gut instincts or your hypothesis on a question, idea or concept you find quite interesting? Two might not pan out but one just might! All it takes is one good one! How about a lot of action…**NOW?**

IT'S YOUR TIME

In the comic strip *Prism* used his *Powers* of *Borrow It,* *Elaborate* and *Make New Combinations* to **Take a Break and Incubate** and quiet **The Junk Yard Dog**. He sparked the family to go on an excursion and use a decision grid to produce novel and feasible ideas/idea combinations to solve their prioritized issues. He demonstrated that we can choose to think, perceive and respond in fresh and unique ways, and not simply be creatures of habit. By doing so proved, once again that **Imagination will Prevail!**

It's Your Time to resume your journey on the road to your Dream. *Snap back* and elevate your energy, your powerhouse and *work out* with **Take an Excursion or 2** and **Hit 'Em Again**. When you generate an abundance of novel and feasible ideas/idea combinations you blaze your own trail with confidence in order to *Lean into Risk, Embrace Your Dream and Take Proactive Actions to go get it!*

EPISODE II, IMAGINATION WILL PREVAIL!
BATTLE #3

BURST IN HERE WHEN...

You have **Rained and Selected** your Hit Yes Ideas, want to **Take a Break and Incubate** on them, and then **Rain** even more ideas and idea combinations. Then **Select** those that naturally rise to the top!

AND FIGHT OFF THE JUNK-YARD DOG WHO USES THE RESISTORS OF

- **Thinking, Perceiving and Responding in Habit-Bound Ways**

POWER SOURCES

- **Hit Yes Ideas**

...PRISM

THE JUNK-YARD DOG

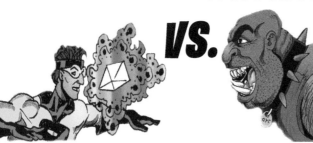

VS.

POWERS

- Borrow It
- Elaborate
- Make New Connections

KEY ACTIONS

- Take a Break and Incubate

WORKOUTS

- Take an Excursion or 2
- Hit 'Em Again

OUTCOMES

MORE HIT YES IDEAS!

IMAGINATION WILL PREVAIL

TAKE A BREAK AND INCUBATE

Burst in here when...you have Rained and Selected your **Hit Yes Ideas**, want to Take a Break and Incubate on them and then Rain even **More Hit Yes Ideas**. From there, converge and select those that naturally rise to the top and best satisfy the criteria!

⒟IVERGENT WORKOUT

TAKE AN EXCURSION OR 2

When you Take an Excursion or 2 you diverge, take a road trip, remove yourself from the current problem/opportunity and experience something that is different (related or unrelated) from your problem/opportunity. You then return to your problem/opportunity, use the stimulus from the excursion and force-connect it to generate novel and spicy ideas. Take the following steps:

- Step away from the problem/opportunity—forget about it for now.
- Take an Excursion or 2, somewhere or something that is different from the problem/opportunity at hand. Use the primer Set of *Excursions* for destination ideas.
- Choose an Excursion or 2 to take and populate those in the (Novel & Spicy Ideas Rack) *Excursions Column*.

Set of Excursions

Acoustics	Adventure	Aeronautics	Africa	Agriculture
Animal Kingdom	Archeology	Art	Arts & Crafts	Astrology
Astronomy	Biblical Times	Biology	Botany	Bridges
Buildings	Cartoons	Celebrations	Child Rearing	Cinema
Comedy	Computers	Cooking	Cosmetology	Crime and Punishment

Dance	Economics	Education	Electricity	Entertainment
Espionage	Exploration	Farming	Fashion and Clothing	Fiction
Finance	Folklore	Forestry	Games	Gardening
Geology	Health and Fitness	History	Imitations	Illusions
Industrial Revolution	Interior Decoration	The Jetsons	Kingdoms	Law and Order
Love and Romance	Machines	Magic	Marriage	Media
Medicine	Metalworking	Minerals	Music	Mythology
Nature	Noise	Nursing	Oceans	Philanthropy
Philosophy	Physics	Plants	Politics	Sales and Marketing
Science	Shopping	Smells	Sports	Theatre and Drama
Time	Transportation	Tribes and Customs	Vacations	War
Weather	Wild West	Woodworking	Yosemite	Zoology

- List the attributes associated with the *Excursion(s)* and populate these in the *Excursion Attributes Column.*
- Return to the problem/opportunity at hand. Working with one attribute at a time, ask: *'How can I use this attribute to help solve my problem/ opportunity? What ideas does this give me?'* Populate these in the *Novel, Spicy Ideas Column.*
- Bring forward the Hit Yes Ideas from the previous **Reverse the Hidden Assumptions Workout** and combine these with your list.

Novel & Spicy Idea Rack

Excursions	Excursion Attributes	Novel, Spicy Ideas (from Take an Excursion or 2)	Novel Spicy Ideas (from Reverse the Hidden Assumptions)

You **Rained** a bountiful quantity of novel and spicy ideas to solve the problem/opportunity at hand. It's time to converge, **Hit 'Em Again** and select the ideas that rise to the top and best meet the criteria. After all, this isn't your first rodeo.

CONVERGENT WORKOUT

HIT 'EM AGAIN

When you **Hit 'Em Again** you converge and use the Decision Selection Grid to select the idea options that rise to the top and best satisfy the criteria. **Note: With this version of the grid, we've added a twist so you can apply weighted criteria.** Use the following steps:

- Identify the criteria to judge your idea options and list them across the top row labeled *Criteria*. Ensure the criteria are as specific as possible.
- Assign weight to the criteria according to its relative importance using a scale of 1/low – 5/high. Place the values in the row titled Weight, under the criteria.
- List the idea options in the column directly below *Idea Options*.
- Working with one idea option at a time moving from left to right, rate each idea to the degree it meets the criteria using a scale of 1/ meets – 3/fully meets. Follow the same process for each idea option.
- Multiply the rating in each cell by the value associated with the criteria. This will yield the overall score for each idea option.
- Add up the weighted scores for the idea options. The options with the highest scores best meet the overall decision criteria.
- If warranted, generate ways to strengthen the idea options with low ratings.

Decision Selection Grid

Criteria								
Weight (1-5)								
	Score (1-3)							
Idea Options								**Total**

Summary of Episode ii, Imagination will Prevail, Battle #3: Prism Quiets The Junk Yard Dog.

After you primed the pump with many tips, tricks, tools, techniques and a comic strip to liberate your *B e y o n d e r Powers*, you burst in with your Hit Yes Ideas, collaborated with *Prism* and used your *Powers* of *Borrow It, Elaborate* and *Make New Connections* to **Take a Break and Incubate**. You *worked out* with **Take an Excursion or 2** and **Hit 'Em Again** to generate even More Hit Yes Ideas! You now have a workbench of ideas to work from to cobble together a Best Concept/Prototype!

Glimpse forward to Imagination will Prevail, Battle #4: Plusser Strikes Fear into The 3 Headed Gremlin

You will burst in with More Hit Yes Ideas, collaborate with *Plusser*, use your *Powers* of *Put Ideas in Context, Evaluate and Select It* and *Strengthen It* to **Strengthen the Concept**. Your outcome will be a Best Concept/Prototype! See if anyone can keep up, I doubt that they can!

MAKE A TWO-BOARD ADJUSTMENT

Get rid of your Gotta Gotta do's

Change the game and reclaim back precious time by ridding yourself from the painful affliction of the gotta gotta do's. Take the following actions:

1. Make a list of your gotta gotta do's.
2. Sketch a four column table. Label the 1st column, gotta, gotta do's; the 2nd column Stop; the 3rd column Start and the 4th column Continue.
3. Working with each gotta gotta do at a time, ask: 'What if I Stop doing this task, what would be the impact?' If low, put a check next to it. Cease and desist with this task and walk away forever from this task tyranny.
4. If the impact is moderate – high ask: 'Do I personally need to do this task?' 'Could I delegate it or find a more effective way to do it?' For these tasks, put a check next to it and then find a way to delegate or devise a more effective way of doing it.
5. The purpose of Start is to start doing tasks that will have moderate – high impact, but you are not currently doing, or doing enough of (e.g. exercising, developing key relationships, strengthening skills, etc.). Be judicious, less is more. Add one at a time and see where it takes you.

3 HEADS ARE NOT BETTER THAN 1

Decide whether or not the goal is worth the risks involved.
If it is, stop worrying.

— Amelia Earhart, first female aviator to fly solo across the Atlantic Ocean

OH MY GOODNESS, IT'S NOT SAFE UP HERE

The Low V is a trust-building exercise conducted on a team-building ropes course. Visualize two diverging cables at waist height that are suspended in a V. In pairs, each person stands on one of the cables, face-to-face with the other person on the opposite cable. Each pair has to *lean in,* clasp hands and work together, accompanied by the spotters underneath them to traverse the cable towards the widest part of the V. As you traverse down the cable, you and your partner need to lean in further which demands that you trust them and the spotters, otherwise you will fall into the open V. At the widest part of the V, you and your partner are virtually horizontal, pushing against each other, holding each other up. Success demands you have trust in yourself, your partner and the spotters. It is visceral.

Round two, the High V is the same exercise as the Low V with three differences. *You and your partner are*: (1) 30 feet up in the air; (2) sporting a climbing harness; (3) supported by *belayers* on the ground. Belaying is a technique used on a climber to exert or release tension on a climbing rope. The belayers keep a close eye on the climber and help them maneuver by letting out slack in the line and release the belay (a device that locks and releases the rope). There are no nets to catch you, but they aren't needed because of the way the belay system is engineered, plus the spotting assistance provided by the belayers. Mirroring the Low V event, success requires trust in yourself, your partner and the belayers. It is the identical exercise as the Low V yet is a very different visceral experience being 30 feet up in the air. Emotions run a little wild. John Medina (2014), affiliate professor of bioengineering at University of Washington School of Medicine, explains: "*Emotions are automatic, largely unconscious behavioral and cognitive responses triggered when the brain detects a positively or negatively charged significant stimulus.*"

Of the two events, the Low V, is actually more dangerous because you and your partner aren't sporting a harness and aren't being belayed in an engineered system. Most people think the High V is more dangerous because of the height factor. In the High V event, we tell ourselves we are not safe because we are 30 feet in the air, but the perception isn't supported by the facts. *Fear and the perception of fear* are powerful human emotions and they can be debilitating.

Come on down from the High V to the workplace. A recent Gallup American Workplace Survey (Wigert, Robinson, 2018) of over 16,500 employees found that three foundational factors are needed to foster creativity in the workplace, and unfortunately are not always prevalent:

- Time to be creative
- Expectations to be creative at work
- Freedom to take the risks necessary to be creative

With respect to risk taking, only 18 percent of employees *strongly agreed* when asked if they are able to take risks at work that could lead to important new products, services or solutions.

On one side of the coin we have risk taking: boldness, adventure, fearlessness, taking a gamble, experimenting and going out on a limb. On the other side is fear: failing, being wrong, uncertainty, rejection, ambiguity, not being in control, not fitting in, being reprimanded and possible humiliation! A primary barrier to creativity in the workplace, as well as in life is the emotion (or perception) of fear to take risks and accept the resultant consequences. *'What if I fail?' 'What if I make a fool of myself?' 'What if my idea isn't accepted?' 'What if I'm ostracized?'* When this takes hold, creativity and innovation become frozen solid in their tracks. We lose twice when we don't foster a climate of risk taking and:

- We don't capitalize on opportunities that we or our fellow associates may already see.
- We create a climate of insecurity for people to work in.

Let's peel back a few layers of the fear onion and take a look at: (1) the fear of failure and the need to be right; (2) the fear of ambiguity and the need to be in control; (3) the fear of rejection and the need to fit in.

FEAR OF FAILURE AND THE NEED TO BE RIGHT

There's nothing wrong with being afraid. And true courage is not, not being afraid. True courage is being afraid, and going ahead and doing your job anyhow, that's what courage is.

— General H. Norman Schwarzkopf, Commander,
Operation Desert Storm

If I have the need to always be right, then I fear failure. It's simply not possible to be right and avoid failure when we are in unfamiliar territory and looking to blaze new trails and approaches. Thomas Edison soundly underscored this point. Albeit it can feel counterintuitive, the faster we accelerate our experiments when in unfamiliar territory, the sooner we get to actually being right and minimizing failure. We often go to great lengths to avoid failure. Failure can mean many different things, for example:

- Realizing you aren't living your life the way you want to.
- Not succeeding in your plans and reaching your goals.
- Finding yourself vulnerable or in the extreme, being close to rock-bottom.

Failure and being wrong are personal, ambiguous and subjective terms because people view them differently. What counts as failure is very personal and may be the polar opposite for someone else. To some, failure and being wrong is a necessary trial and error method  to learn and try a different approach. It doesn't represent an end but can serve as a stepping-stone. For others, a main fear of failing and being wrong comes with the disappointment that follows. Despite the effort, things didn't go as you wanted them to go, and it evokes an emotion such that you might decide not to put yourself out there again. That is why for many, the fear of failure can be the worst fear of all.

The fear of failure is frequently used as an excuse to procrastinate, or to not take actions to make a situation better. *"Why bother? I'm just not up to it or good enough."* Or conversely, if the work environment is perceived not to be idea-friendly, trusting or collaborative, and if I must win and cannot fail…I will rig things so that I will win. How many times have you heard the proclamation, *"We want our people to fail fast?"* Failing fast is a good practice if it is real and not an empty and destructive bumper sticker slogan. People see through it fast.

FEAR OF AMBIGUITY AND THE NEED TO BE IN CONTROL

To bring about change, you must not be afraid to take the first step.
We will fail when we fail to try.

— Rosa Parks, Civil Rights activist

If I feel I must always be in control then I fear ambiguity, the unknown and disappointment. I may fear someone else being in control, or worse yet, someone else getting the credit. I must know what is waiting for me around the corner because if I don't know, I'm not able to control or manipulate the situation. And if I don't like what is different or changing, it is simply because I either don't understand it, or have a plan to control it beforehand.

The fear of disappointment is a good part of the reason we avoid the unknown. When we disappoint other people or experience disappointment ourselves, we are dissatisfied because our expectations did not match the results of what actually happened. We make our best effort to avoid disappointment because it is a negative feeling and can be followed by regret, where we wonder if our choices contributed to the outcome. We ask, *"If I had done things differently, would it have made a difference?"* This fear of the unknown can grind our progress to a standstill, which makes it doubly hard for us to discover and understand new things. It becomes a self-defeating prophecy where we train ourselves to expect rejection and as a result to not be open-minded.

The paradox is that when we look to innovate, we are right smack in the middle of ambiguity, in the land of not knowing (*oh my goodness, it's the ranger, what will we do?*). How could we be anywhere else for goodness sakes, when what we're thinking to build hasn't been invented yet! This is high voltage, ambiguous terrain. You can't know the results because they aren't certain. We simply can't be in control of or wire the outcome, it's not possible. However, what we can be in control of is our attitude, in how we choose to meet ambiguity and the uncertainty of whatever life hands us.

FEAR OF REJECTION AND THE NEED TO FIT IN

If you fall during your life, it doesn't matter.
You're never a failure if you try to get up.

— Evel Knievel, stunt performer and entertainer

If I must absolutely fit in, I fear rejection. Feelings of emptiness are in some way caused by the absence of interaction, or from non-optimal interactions with other people. These fears have evolved from our early survival instincts. We fear rejection and loneliness because we think it is more likely that we would survive if we live in a group. The fear of rejection and loneliness are also related to doing something and no one noticing. We can feel that for our actions to be meaningful, someone must notice them.

If we suffer from the social fear of not projecting a good image to other people, we can negatively interpret receiving constructive criticism. We may even interpret it as ridicule and rejection. Take public speaking for example. Many people fear public speaking because it can be a lonely place. The thought of having to speak in front of an audience can signal our sweat glands to swing wide open and release balls of sweat on our back that travel northward, defying gravity and soaking our nicely pressed shirts and blouses. At the same time our mouth experiences the opposite sensation, becoming a desert. Did someone say *cottonmouth*? We have all experienced *stage fright* at least once in our lives. And what is it that we fear? We fear we might forget our lines, hose it up and give the audience a reason to respond negatively, laugh (wasn't trying to be funny), boo, throw things, go quiet, not pay attention or be indifferent. No one likes being in the spotlight negatively. We fear not fitting in, being lonely or being rejected because we often justify our contributions through the acknowledgment and acceptance of others. And similar to the fears of failure and ambiguity, when we are in the choppy, unchartered waters of creativity and innovation, *it is virtually impossible to perfectly fit in.* Can't be certain of how deep or cold the water is when standing on the shore. Kind of like when Tonto, the sidekick of The Lone Ranger said, *"What's this we Kemosabe?"*

LURKING IN THE SHADOWS

Many issues connected to fear *lurk in the shadows of organizations.* They are there, oh yes, but are not readily talked about because people fear they will be tagged as not being a *'team player.'* We can have obedient team players yet very little creativity and innovation. Or we can give the innovation pot a real good stirring and **fan the hot blue flames** and get the sparks-a-flying with different combinations of individual contributors and teams. It's up to you to experiment with a variety of potent combinations.

Ah yes, if the work climate is not idea-friendly and affirming **The 3 Headed Gremlin** will rear its' three ugly heads time after time. And what are the consequences? What does a climate of fear cost an individual, team or organization in lost opportunities? What is the impact of less than optimal team alignment and collaboration? Following are a few visible symptoms:

- Turf battles between functional groups.
- Not studying problems/opportunities jointly and learning together.
- Having too many handoffs — throwing it over the wall to the other department.
- Not tightly time-boxing initiatives and allowing them to go on for way too long, losing valuable and non-replaceable time.
- People harboring ideas and continually jockeying for position to take the credit.
- Not fostering a climate that brings out the best in other people.
- Being too overly process-focused where it suffocates imaginative thinking.
- Momentum getting sucked into the quicksand with far too many meetings, reviews, cooks in the kitchen and speed bump decision points.

Some managers applaud themselves by employing teams for innovation. And while there are positive advantages to teams, they can also create a bureaucracy that is an unintended consequence. In the extreme, it can create a stifling climate that isn't entrepreneurial. Just the opposite may be created, one that is overly process-focused and risk averse, flowing in the opposite direction of innovation. Finding the right balance of teaming and individual efforts is key, one where team members are comfortable and can toggle between operating as a minority of one and in a team.

What do you think would happen to fear in a climate where people first genuinely look to strengthen ideas and concepts; find the potential in them, and to not prematurely criticize them? What is the power of possible – the sheer strength of an idea affirming climate? Having a sprinter's speed is quite a valuable asset. And possibly even more valuable is having explosive strength. Sounds to me like it may very well be just the right time to bring in *The B e y o n d e r* who has explosive strengthening on her mind…

MAKE A TWO-BOARD ADJUSTMENT

Integrate Just-In-Time Resources and Time Box It

Just-In-Time Resources need to be available when required *(e.g.* sketch and graphic artists, engineers, facilitators, technical experts and consultants; access to leadership, information; sufficient budget for excursion expenses (e.g., gasoline for the VW van, comic books, gum, beef jerky, pickled eggs and Mountain Dew).

Time boxing imposes a fixed amount of time to conduct tasks and the discipline to stick to it. It is a powerful antidote to *Parkinson's Law* (work expands to fill the time available for its completion). If for example, you give yourself three days to complete a one hour task, then it will increase in complexity to fill the three days. The time period you allot to develop solutions should be compressed. If you have *Rained Ideas* and *Hit 'em,* then impose a goal to not exceed one hour to develop a first cut back of the envelope concept/solution.

...PLUSSER

has the unique *Power* to cobble together and **Strengthen the Concept**. She does this by taking the *Hit Yes Ideas* from her sidekicks *Micro-Burst* and *Prism* and cobbles them together into an actionable concept/prototype. She then finds the plusses and potentials in the concept, uses *goal wishing* to identify the drawbacks and generates options to overcome them. The outcome she produces is a Best Concept/Prototype. And by doing so, she can boldly proclaim that **Imagination will Prevail.**

Her *Powers* are:

Put Ideas in Context

- Put ideas and concepts into a big, wide angle picture context.
- Synthesize ideas and cobble them together into an organized concept.
- Communicate the essence of a concept by showing its relationship to something that is known, understood and valued by other people.
- Quantify the economic value of a concept even if it is difficult to do so.

Evaluate and Select It

- Pay attention to what your logic, emotions and intuition say to you.
- Think critically and use criteria to help deduce sound conclusions.
- Compare, contrast and make decisions on the appropriateness, value and difficulty among competing alternatives.
- Choose options that you believe will achieve a solid return, and not have a daunting amount of difficulty to implement.

Strengthen It

- Identify the plusses and potential of ideas and concepts by first listening for what's right about them.
- Use goal-wishing (I wish) to generate options to overcome the drawbacks of ideas and concepts.
- Give ideas and concepts a fair hearing and don't be hasty in making decisions prematurely.
- Develop problem-prevention actions to minimize the probability and negate the impact of factors that could derail implementing a concept/prototype.

STRENGTHEN THE CONCEPT

It is impossible to live without failing at something unless you live so cautiously that you might as well not have lived at all – in which case you fail by default.

— J.K. Rowling, British author

PROPEL ON DOWN FROM THE HIGH V

Propel on down from the High V, look risk straight in the eye and stare it down. Ask, "*In what ways can I prime the pump, grease the skids and reduce the friction to significantly increase my and/or the team's innovation productivity?*" You can wait for the moment to arrive, or you can be bold and increase your odds of success by taking decisive action to foster an idea affirming, creative climate. A good percentage of our time spent in organizations is working in small teams. The work climate affects the creative production of individuals and teams, either positively or negatively. You can have creative individuals, yet their creative production can be stymied as a result of ineffective management work practices, and yes, the F E A R of risk-taking.

FOSTER A RISK-TAKING, CREATIVE CLIMATE

Risks I like to say always pay off. You learn what to do or what not to do.

— Jonas Salk, M.D. Developer of the Polio Vaccine

We can't always control all the factors that affect creative production, yet why not reach back, grab the wheel, and give it a damn good spin just for the sport of it? Swedish creativity researcher Goran Ekvall (1996) identified ten *'creative climate'* dimensions that impact creativity in teams/organizations (nine positively and one negatively correlated). This list provides a set of levers we have at our disposal to increase creative productivity.

- **Goal & Challenge**: The degree to which a person/team has well-defined and meaningful goals, challenges and assignments. Most people are motivated by big goals and challenges.

- **Autonomy**: The amount of time and latitude people have to pursue ideas to solve the challenge and meet the goals.

- **Idea Support**: This defines how new ideas are treated. The climate needs to be new-idea friendly, and not hostile or ambivalent.

- **Trust and Openness**: The degree of trust and openness people have in their relationships with other people. This impacts how readily they share novel thinking and ideas.

- **Dynamism and Liveliness**: How much positive electricity is in the environment; how vibrant and engaging is the climate? Can you feel it?

- **Playfulness and Humor**: The amount of idea playfulness people exhibit with new ideas and possibilities. Can you feel and see joyfulness, humor and spontaneous interactions?

- **Debates and Conflict**: With healthy debates and conflict, people passionately share their ideas and views even when they differ from their peers. With negative debates and conflict (the negatively correlated dimension) differences in viewpoints aren't readily shared or accepted and the climate is stifling. Hello, groupthink!

- **Idea Time:** A portion of free time each day to pursue new and fresh thinking — freed up from the demands of the current tasks at hand.

- **Risk Taking:** The degree to which risk-taking is truly valued, encouraged and supported. It's not a slogan or a bumper sticker. Embracing uncertainty and ambiguity are the norm. Risk-taking is aligned with experimentation, testing new questions, ideas and alternatives.

"Can't we just get along with one another?" While cooperation is a good thing, a more robust question is: "How to tap into and leverage the collective talents of people?" ***Synergy*** describes the creation of a whole that is greater than the sum of its parts. Achieving synergistic levels of collaboration between people is the goal—to make it the norm—not the exception.

What happens in the brain during musical improvisation? Dr. Charles Limb (2020) a surgeon, neuroscientist and musician at the University of

California has used Magnetic Resonance Image technology to study musicians to see what happens in their brains when they freestyle and improvise. Results showed that when musicians are creating something new, parts of the brain associated with the senses and motor regions that govern self-expression (language and visual imagery) are more active and light up. Interestingly, another part of the brain associated with inhibition, self-monitoring and self-awareness quiets down, which enables creative, free-flowing output. As a musician, if you are thinking about what could happen if you make mistakes, then you take fewer risks and impede the goal of generating novel, free-flowing music. You effectively shut down the new generative impulses.

USE YES, AND

Dogs have a lot to communicate to a person willing to listen.

— Susan Butcher, a pioneer in dog-sled racing and
four-time winner of the Iditarod

How about we borrow a few principles of improvisation to foster an idea-affirming creative climate? Improvisation you ask? Improvisation is comedy that basically creates something out of nothing. It is spontaneous, free-flowing and is a group (at least two) effort. The script is provided by the audience or the moderator (no script to study, memorize or practice in advance); stuff happens (the act is right now, in the moment); and you have to collaborate together and make it up on the spot. There is no one else to lean on. It represents a both/and situation versus an either/or. Following are three principles we can borrow from improvisation to foster a strong idea affirming climate (Leonard & Yorton, 2015):

- *Principle #1 — **Accept the Offer** (The Yes)*
- *Principle #2 — **Advance the Offer** (The And)*
- *Principle #3 — **Make Your Partner Look Good** (The Why Not?)*

Accept the Offer **(The Yes)**. With the attitude of **Yes** we accept the gift of the offer. When we hear the offer, we don't judge it; we *defer judgment*. Some gifts aren't wrapped well: the corners aren't tight, too much tape is used, it doesn't have a pretty bow or trendy ribbon and isn't color-coordinated.

So what? They are still gifts. It is our responsibility to hear and accept the offer, the gift. To accept and hear the offer we need to stop talking so much *and listen much* (we have twice as many ears as tongues, might just as well use 'em)! Effective improvisers aren't necessarily more quick-witted or clever than their peers, they happen to listen really well. They hear the gift their partners offer. That's mighty tough to do when you are thinking about the idea you want to talk about instead of listening to the idea your partner is trying to share with you.

Advance the Offer **(The And)**. With the **Yes**, we accept the gift of the offer. With **The And**, we connect to the gift, *build on it and advance it*. The attitude of **The And** is *to tune into the gift being offered* with the intent to do something positive with it — to advance it, make it stronger and give it legs. No, we don't judge or criticize it. Yes, we are fully present, tuned in and engaged with **The And**. Doing so, we foster an idea-affirming climate and we encourage our counterpart to create the future *together*.

Make Your Partner Look Good **(The Why Not?)**. To build on **The Yes** and **The And**, let go of the need to control the situation. We really can't fully control anything anyways. At a minimum all we can do is influence things. Stop stressing and focusing your energy on what you are going to do to react, what you are going to say next. Jump into and stay in the flow to *Make Your Partner Look Good* in the process. The flow is where the creative productivity occurs, so might as well put your energy in the flow to *Make your Partner Look Good* and make yourself look good too. **Why not?**

Yes, And is a most powerful and virtuous attitude that embodies humility, sincerity and courage. It affirms our human spirit, boldest dreams, and the spirit and dreams of others. Adopting this powerful idea-affirming and collaborative attitude is certainly a risk worth leaning into and taking, don't you think?

MAKE A TWO-BOARD ADJUSTMENT

Teach Other People to be Creative

You learn how to be creative at a deeper level
when you teach it. Average athletes tend to
become better coaches because they had to
learn the subtleties of the game and couldn't
rely on pure athleticism. With teaching, you
have to pay attention to the little things
and when you teach them you learn
again at a deeper level.

Speaking of trumping fear, I've got a sneaking suspicion that a very devious **Resistor** is going to get a good taste of his own lousy, foul tasting medicine…

BATTLE #4

...PLUSSER
STRIKES FEAR INTO
THE 3 HEADED GREMLIN

THE 3 HEADED GREMLIN

Her *Powers* are:

- *Put Ideas in Context*
- *Evaluate and Select It*
- *Strengthen It*

Emotional Resistors

- **Fear of Failure**
- **Fear of Ambiguity**
- **Fear of Rejection**

TO BE CONTINUED...

EPISODE PROFILE:
SALLY RIDE

I've been a bit of a risk-taker all of my life.

— Dr. Sally Ride, first American woman in space

Source, Google Images

Dr. Sally Ride was completing her Ph.D. studies in physics, astrophysics and English at Stanford University when she responded to the National Aeronautics and Space Administration (NASA), which was recruiting applicants for the astronaut corps.

Throughout the Mercury, Gemini and Apollo space flight programs, NASA had recruited astronauts solely from military test pilots, and access was closed to women. In 1978 NASA began recruiting scientists for the Space Shuttle program. Dr. Ride, along with 8,000 other applicants, responded to the ad. She was accepted into the astronaut training program along with 35 other people, including five women. Over the next year, she trained in a regimen that included parachute jumping, water survival, gravity and weightlessness training, radio communications, navigation and flight instruction.

On June 18, 1983 Dr. Ride became the first American woman and youngest American astronaut at the age of 32, to fly in space as a crew member on the Shuttle mission STS-7. Over the six-day mission the five-person crew deployed two communications satellites and conducted a number of pharmaceutical and material experiments. Dr. Ride was the first woman to use the shuttle's robotic arm in space to retrieve a satellite.

Dr. Ride returned to space on October 5, 1984 as a mission specialist on Challenger STS-41-G. During the eight-day mission the crew launched communication satellites using large format cameras to observe the earth and used a new technique to refuel satellites in orbit. Over her two missions Dr. Ride logged more than 343 hours in space.

Dr. Ride had completed eight months of training for her third flight, STS-61-M, when on January 28, 1986 the Challenger disaster occurred and the entire crew perished in the catastrophe. Plans and preparation for further missions were immediately suspended.

Dr. Ride subsequently was named to the Rogers Commission (the presidential commission investigating the Challenger explosion and the 2003 Columbia crash). Following the investigation, she worked at NASA headquarters and led NASA's strategic planning effort. She authored a report, "NASA Leadership and America's Future in Space", and founded NASA's Office of Exploration.

After her career at NASA, Dr. Ride worked at the Center for International Security and Arms Control at Stanford University, was a professor of physics at the University of California, San Diego, and director of the California Space Institute. From the mid-1990s until her death, Dr. Ride led two public-outreach programs for NASA, the ISS EarthKAM and the GRAIL MoonKAM in cooperation with NASA's Jet Propulsion Laboratory and UCSD. The programs allowed middle school students to request images of the Earth and Moon.

Dr. Ride was also an inspiration for young girls to reach for the stars, especially in science, math and technology. She wrote six science books for children and founded Sally Ride Science to make science and engineering 'cool again', providing science-oriented school programs and teacher training. Dr. Ride **felt comfortable as a minority of one**. She was a trailblazer as the first American woman in space. What courage, determination, smarts and set of accomplishments.

A Provocative Question: How to look past the barriers in your life (real or imagined) and truly **reach for that shining star**? The sky is not the limit. Sally Ride broke the *atmospheric glass ceiling*.

IT'S YOUR TIME

In the comic strip *Plusser* used her *Powers* of *Put Ideas in Context, Evaluate and Select It* and *Strengthen It* to **Strengthen the Concept** and Strike Fear into **The 3 Headed Gremlin** and **The Junk Yard Dog**. She helped the family cobble together and strengthen a Best Concept/Prototype. And yes, she proved for a third time's the charm that **Imagination will Prevail**!

It's Your Time to put the pedal to the metal, punch your velocity and **Strengthen the Concept**. It's time to really get moving and *work out* with **Cobble 'Em Together, Use the Back of the Napkin** and **Strengthen It** to build on your Hit Yes Ideas and develop a Best Concept/Prototype. Get in the pole position so you can *Lean into Risk, Embrace Your Dream and Take Proactive Actions to go get it!*

EPISODE II, IMAGINATION WILL PREVAIL! BATTLE #4

BURST IN HERE WHEN...

You have selected your Hit Yes Ideas, want to cobble them together into an organized, actionable concept and then strengthen it to be a Best Concept/Prototype.

AND FIGHT OFF THE THREE HEADED GREMLIN AND HIS EMOTIONAL RESISTORS

- Fear of Failure
- Fear of Ambiguity
- Fear of Rejection

POWER SOURCES

- More Hit Yes Ideas

THE 3 HEADED GREMLIN VS. ...PLUSSER

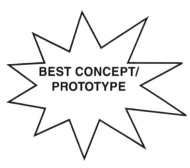

POWERS

- Put Ideas in Context
- Evaluate and Select It
- Strengthen It

KEY ACTIONS

- Strengthen the Concept

WORKOUTS

- Cobble 'Em Together
- Use the Back of the Napkin
- Strengthen It

OUTCOMES

BEST CONCEPT/ PROTOTYPE

IMAGINATION WILL PREVAIL

STRENGTHEN THE CONCEPT

Burst in here when...you have selected your More Hit Yes Ideas, want to cobble them together into an organized, actionable concept and then strengthen it to be a Best Concept/Prototype!

©ONVERGENT WORKOUT

COBBLE 'EM TOGETHER

When you **Cobble 'Em Together** you converge, start with your More Hit Yes Ideas and cobble them together into an organized, actionable concept/prototype. Use the following steps:

- Bring forward your More Hit Yes Ideas from **Take a Break and Incubate** and populate them in the chart following.
- Working with one idea or group of similar ideas at a time, ask: *"What does each idea/group of ideas mean to me? What does each idea/ group of ideas represent?"*
- Working from your responses, ask, *'What action do I now see taking?'*

More Hit Yes Ideas	Action
Idea # 1 represents…	The action I now see taking is…
Idea # 2 represents…	The action I now see taking is…
Idea # 3 represents…	The action I now see taking is…

Idea # 4 represents...	The action I now see taking is...
Idea # 5 represents...	The action I now see taking is...
Idea # 6 represents...	The action I now see taking is...
Idea # 7 represents...	The action I now see taking is...

Review your responses and cobble together a 1st cut organized, actionable concept/prototype (bullet points are fine). A little drum-roll please:

'The organized, actionable concept/prototype I now see implementing is....'

Now, segue and **Use the Back of the Napkin** to refine your concept/prototype.

MAKE A TWO-BOARD ADJUSTMENT

Set Meaningful Daily Quotas

Successful writers set daily quotas to write a certain amount of words. Successful athletes set daily exercise quotas/regimens of exercises and number of repetitions. Do the same. Depending on where you are in your process, set daily quotas for either problem statements, novel ideas, feasible ideas, concepts, prototypes and implementation actions…and hit them.

©ONVERGENT WORKOUT

USE THE BACK OF THE NAPKIN

When you **Use the Back of the Napkin** you take the output from **Cobble 'Em Together**, converge and refine your concept/prototype. Use the following questions:

What is the name of the concept?	What is the lead news story headline? Explain your concept in 1–2 sentences:
What problem or opportunity does your concept solve for your customer? Who is the customer? What is their central problem or opportunity?	**How does the concept work?** Describe in sufficient detail how the concept works and how it solves the customer's problem or opportunity. What is the evidence that the concept will solve the problem or opportunity?
What is unique about this concept? Explain how this concept is truly unique and isn't just 'more of the same.'	**What is the concept worth?** To the customer? To you?

What do you estimate the concept (or prototype) will cost to develop (time, $, resources)?	Where is the quicksand? Where could this concept get sucked into the quicksand, get stuck or derailed?
How to avoid the quicksand? What ideas are needed to avoid the quicksand?	**How to test the concept with users?** How to test your concept/prototype with users?

"The concept/prototype I now see implementing is...."

Propel forward with your concept/prototype and **Strengthen It**!

IMAGINATION WILL PREVAIL

STRENGTHEN THE CONCEPT

Burst in here when...you have cobbled together an actionable, organized concept and want to strengthen it to be a Best Concept/Prototype!

CONVERGENT WORKOUT

STRENGTHEN IT

When you **Strengthen It**, you converge and strengthen your concept to be a Best Concept/Prototype. When you are in a strengthening frame of mind you have *zero time* to be fearful, you don't try to overcome your fears because you aren't even thinking about them. They aren't relevant because you are focused on strengthening your concept. This mindset trumps fear, defeating thoughts and the strengthened concept will prevail. Use the following steps:

- Focus in on what's right about your concept by listing **3 plusses** of it. Ask *"What's right about it right now?"*

  - "The 1st plus I see with the concept is…"
  - "The 2nd plus I see with the concept is…"
  - "The 3rd plus I see with the concept is…"

- Identify **3 potentials** of the concept. Ask *"In the future when it has become a reality what is the potential of it?"*

  - "The 1st potential I see with the concept is…"
  - "The 2nd potential I see with the concept is…"
  - "The 3rd potential I see with the concept is…"

- Identify the **drawbacks** of the concept. Regardless of how strong the concept may be there are always drawbacks. For each drawback, use the goal wishing language: *"I wish there was a way…"*

  - "The 1st drawback I see with the concept is…" "I wish there was a way…"
  - "The 2nd drawback I see with the concept is…" "I wish there was a way…"
  - "The 3rd drawback I see with the concept is…" "I wish there was a way…"

- Review your drawbacks and wishes. Rub the lamp and generate ideas to have each wish granted and populate them in the following chart. Work from the most important to least important. Continue until you have generated a sufficient number of ideas to have all of your wishes granted (we received a waiver on the 3 wish limit from the Genie).

Grant Wishing Ideas

Drawback # 1: Wish # 1:	Drawback # 2: Wish # 2:	Drawback # 3: Wish # 3:
Grant Wishing Ideas	Grant Wishing Ideas	Grant Wishing Ideas

- Review your plusses, potentials and grant-wishing ideas. Cobble these together to make your concept a Best Concept/Prototype! Could we have a little drum roll here please…

- *"The Best Concept/Prototype I now see implementing is…"*

Summary of Episode ii, Imagination will Prevail, Battle #4: Plusser Strikes Fear into The 3 Headed Gremlin:

After priming the pump with many tips, tricks, tools, techniques and a comic strip to liberate your *B e y o n d e r Powers*, you burst in with More Hit Yes Ideas, collaborated with *Plusser*, used your *Powers* of *Put Ideas in Context, Evaluate* and *Select It* and *Strengthen It* to Strengthen the Concept. You *worked out* with **Cobble 'Em Together, Use the Back of the**

Napkin and Strengthen It. Your outcome was a Best Concept/Prototype! Now that is something to marvel.

Summary of Episode ii, Imagination will Prevail, Battles #2-4:

You burst in with your Clarified/Prioritized Problem/Opportunity Statements, collaborated with *Micro-Burst, Prism* and *Plusser* and used your *Powers* to **Rain and Select Ideas, Take a Break and Incubate** and **Strengthen the Concept**. Your outcome was a Best Concept/Prototype – one that will win!

Glimpse forward to **Episode iii, The Power of Speed, Battle #5: Momentum Breaks the Grip of The Vice**

You will burst in with your Best Concept/Prototype, collaborate with *Momentum* and use your *Powers* of *Be Optimistic, Use Humor and Intuition* and *Act on It* to **Xcelerate the Momentum** and **Catapult the Energy**. You will *work out* with **Get Fast Traction, Name, Laugh and Shout at It;** and **Adapt and Adjust**. Your outcome will be action plans to implement your Best Concept/Prototype. Here we go Cyclones, here we go!

MAKE A TWO-BOARD ADJUSTMENT

Notice Everyday Things and Events

Take the time to notice everyday things you normally don't. Provoke yourself to notice everyday things on purpose to pique your curiosity. Mentally take on different roles (e.g. pretend to be a detective, author, poet or tourist) and look through these frames to see things as if for the first time. Choose to experience your environment, you world in a newer, richer way.

EPISODE III
THE POWER OF SPEED

SPEED MATTERS

It's your duty to fly the airplane. If you get killed in it, you don't know anything about it anyway. Duty is paramount. It's that simple if you're a military guy. You don't say I'm not going to do that—that's dangerous. If it's your duty to do it, that's the way it is.

— General Chuck Yeager, USAF, first pilot to break the sound barrier

Most commercial aircraft require approximately 2,300 feet to gain enough speed to successfully take off. Contrast that with the flight deck of the United States Navy's Nimitz class aircraft carriers, where the runway is approximately 300 feet long. These ships currently use steam-powered catapults on the decks that are capable of launching fighter jets from 0 to 175 mph in two seconds. *Now that's fast!* So if that isn't fast enough for you speed junkies, the Navy is currently deploying a new Electromagnetic Aircraft Launch System to replace the steam powered catapults with electromagnetic catapults where the fighter jets will be launched from 0 to 150 mph in less than a second (Wright, 2007). *Now that's really, really fast!*

Speed is our guiding principle in **Episode iii**. We want lots of it. We want purposeful action to implement concepts/solutions/prototypes and

to learn from them. We want *to experiment, prototype, learn and adapt fast* to succeed. Time is our most valuable resource. We all have 10,080 minutes per week. We can't create any more, however we can carve out more time for creative work. Our mission is to Break the Iron Grip of **The Vice** and his *Workload Pressure Resistors:*

- **Extreme Time Pressures**
- **Unrealistic Expectations for Creative Productivity**
- **Distractions from Creative Work**

EXTREME TIME PRESSURES

The two most powerful warriors are patience and time.

— Leo Tolstoy, Russian writer who is considered
one of the greatest authors of all time

I wish I had a shiny silver dollar for every time someone has said to me: *"Dan, these creative-thinking practices are effective, they work real good...* **B UT** *I live in the real world and I think you only visit it from time to time. I've got to focus on the fundamentals, the blocking and the tackling. I can't be distracted from my main job. Creativity is a luxury."*

I can hear Sonny and Cher singing, "And the beat goes on, the beat goes on." Those shiny silver dollars would be weighing me down right now—a silver Fort Knox!

EVERYDAY WORK VS. CREATIVE WORK

With *everyday work* we organize tasks and processes to deliver consistent, predictable, reliable and repeatable results. The goal is zero variance. *We want to see old/current things the same way and do our tasks the same way, every time with no exceptions.* We want repeatable tasks. We are focused on high efficiency, productivity and throughput. It is what businesses need to do to make money and be profitable.

Organizing for *creative work* is diametrically opposed to everyday work. Variance is the lifeblood of creativity, so with creative work we want to foster and accelerate variance. We need to be exposed to lots of diverse stimuli to get the hot idea sparks flying. This helps us to break from habit, to think about, perceive and respond differently to things in order to make new connections. *We want to see old/current things in new ways.* A high failure rate is inevitable; in fact, it's necessary. Thomas Edison 'failed' hundreds of times in his attempts to light the incandescent light bulb at an affordable cost. This level of failing is highly problematic in everyday work (you think?). The skills and behaviors that enable high efficiency, productivity and throughput in everyday work are in stark contrast with those required to discover and develop tomorrow's model.

Strolling down memory lane I vividly remember working at a McDonald's restaurant one summer as a teenager and couldn't help peeking into the idea suggestion box on the wall. And sure enough, it was quite lonely. No wonder. Who the heck had time or an incentive to come up with new sandwich ideas or anything else for goodness sakes? This was classic everyday work, we were getting paid (as management consistently reminded us) to get the hamburgers and fries out fast and hot, no exceptions. Do you see all of the people standing in line? They are hungry and are looking kind of mean, don't you think? And heaven forbid if you had any idle time between making the burgers and fries, you were supposed to be wiping down the counters with perpetual Tasmanian Devil motion. Except for me, coming up with new sandwich ideas was the furthest thing from everyone's mind, and I think that's why I didn't stay employed there for the entire summer (darn). In this environment something clearly had to give, and you guessed it, creative work was asked to punch out on the time clock and was reminded not to come back tomorrow, or ever!

MAKE A TWO-BOARD ADJUSTMENT

Schedule Creative Work as Your 1st Task of the Day

How about letting creative work cut the line and make it the most important task of the day? Schedule and knock it out first thing—a focused, energetic 45 minutes integrated with your physical fitness workout—before or after the coffee primer and directly in front of the highly nutritious breakfast! How's that for *Ennnnnnergy?*

COULD USE A BOTH/AND RIGHT ABOUT NOW

You win some, lose some and wreck some.

— Dale Earnhardt, legendary auto racer

Fast forward to today and things have changed, but in some ways not as dramatically as you might think. In the Gallup American Workplace Survey (Wigert, Robinson, 2018) three foundational factors were identified as requirements to foster creativity in the workplace:

1. Time to be creative (have sufficient time and resources to properly engage, get *out of the cube and in the marketplace discovery and ideation process).*
2. Expectations to be creative at work (via established goals, metrics).
3. Freedom to take necessary risks and to be fully supported in the process.

Concerning *time to be creative* 18 percent of employees reported they are given time to be creative only a few times a week; 17 percent reported only a few times a month; and 14 percent reported just a few times a year. Don't think we'll be having a big Fourth of July cookout and fireworks celebration with these numbers. It takes some freeing up from the *day job* to accomplish this because it is difficult to engage in an innovation initiative while simultaneously juggling all the-day-job balls and not have any fall to the ground, unless they are made of rubber.

Creativity Researcher Dr. Teresa Amabile (2002) of the Harvard Business School has written extensively on the factors that support or kill creativity in business. She reported on a multi-year project where her research team investigated the links between time pressure and creativity involving 238 organizational employees across 26 project teams, in seven companies and three industries. The employees filled out an electronic diary every day on their creativity while doing their jobs over the course of their projects. A surprising finding was that employees reported feeling more creative on time-pressured days, even though the data didn't support it. The employees were given evidence of being less creative on those days. Amabile explained:

Overall, very high levels of time pressure should be avoided if you want to foster creativity on a consistent basis. However, if a time crunch is unavoidable, managers can try to preserve creativity by protecting people from fragmentation of their work and distractions. They should also give people a sense of being 'on a mission', doing something difficult but important. I don't think, though, that most people can function effectively in that mode for long periods of time without getting burned out.

If you have the good fortune and a budget to support it, you can organize a team of people to dedicate their full-time efforts on front end fuzzy innovation work to generate new product, process, service and/or business model concepts. Some companies organize their innovation initiatives in this way. Other companies also empower associates to free up some time to work on creative initiatives. In their research report, *Noncommissioned Work* (2012), David Burkus of Oral Roberts University and Gary Oster from Regent University highlight a few leading practices:

- Google has long encouraged its employees to spend 20 percent of their work week focused on side projects.
- 3M is well known for their practices to empower its scientists and engineers to spend up to 15 percent of their time on projects unrelated to their normal work, the only requirement being they have to share their ideas or discoveries with colleagues.
- Australian software company Atlassian has experimented with giving teams 24-hour, autonomous time periods to pursue initiatives not related to their job. They termed the method *FedEx Days* because the teams had to deliver something overnight.
- Twitter launched a concept they dubbed *Hack Week* where engineers are free to reserve an entire week to pursue ideas they find intriguing.

Many organizations have used these concepts, labeled them *discretionary time*, and enabled select employees to free up more modest amounts of time.

If you don't have the budget to support practices like Google and 3M (like just about everyone) the challenge is to find ways to do both/and of everyday work and creative work. Of all the resources we have at our disposal, time is the most precious, is fixed at 1,440 minutes a day and no one gets any more. Okay okay, thanks for sharing, enough already, save some for breakfast tomorrow, will ya? We all live in a time-pressed world, and there never seems to be enough time. Thinking creatively is hard work, it isn't for the faint of heart and it requires putting in the effort. No, the new idea stork doesn't fly on over and drop the new ideas down in a nice tidy basket! And nothing noteworthy will happen if we continue with the convenient excuse cycle of saying there isn't enough time. Rather, how about breaking the cycle, *making the necessary adjustments and making the time for it—smartly?*

Louis Pasteur (2016), a French biologist, chemist and founding father of microbiology, is acclaimed for his discoveries in vaccination, microbial fermentation and the 'the germ theory of disease', which led to pasteurization. He said: "*In the fields of observation, chance favors only the prepared mind.*" This reminds us to carve out sufficient time to prepare, observe and stay open to solving problems with creative solutions. It doesn't happen by chance; hope is not a strategy. It's difficult for novel, valuable questions and ideas to jump into a busy, over-scheduled, *gotta do my gotta do's* mind. You increase the odds of having keen insights when your mind is quiet, ready and prepared. As one of my favorite engineering clients reminds me, "It is an issue of time on task."

UNREALISTIC EXPECTATIONS FOR CREATIVE PRODUCTIVITY

High expectations are the key to everything.

— Sam Walton, Founder of Walmart

As identified in the Gallup American Workplace Survey (Wigert, Robinson, 2018) three foundational factors are needed to foster creativity in the workplace:

1. Time to be creative
2. Expectations to be creative at work
3. Freedom to take the risks necessary to be creative

Concerning the factor of expectations to be creative at work, an underwhelming 29 percent (ouch) of employees responded strongly to the phrase, 'I am expected to be creative or think of new ways to do things at work.'

Setting high expectations for creative productivity demands a positive, can-do attitude. However, if not done well it can be a double-edged sword where you can easily cut yourself and have unfavorable consequences. On one edge of the sword you have positive expectations and specific goals for creativity because these will help drive higher levels of productivity. The Pygmalion effect, also called a self-fulfilling prophecy, kicks in gear here where people will act or behave in a way that others expect them to. If you expect it and inspect it you will get it. When you set expectations for creative productivity it will have a positive influence. You increase the likelihood you will achieve them and this becomes a self-sustaining, self-fulfilling closed loop. You achieve results, build confidence and fuel additional results. Without establishing positive expectations and setting goals nothing big will happen.

On the other edge of the sharp sword are two traps where you can easily cut yourself. *Trap #1 is to establish minimal expectations and goals for creative productivity. Trap #2 is to establish unrealistic expectations for creative productivity.* Trap # 1 also invokes the Pygmalion effect but it's running in the wrong direction because not expecting creative productivity will have a negative influence. You negate the likelihood for creative performance as this too becomes a self-sustaining, self-fulfilling closed loop—going in reverse. If you aren't expressly asked or expected to be creative, you won't be sufficiently challenged, feel the need or feel comfortable doing so. And yell out *bingo* because you virtually guarantee nothing big will happen. With Trap #2, you set yourself and/or the team up for failure right out of the starting blocks. The goals and expectations can be too demanding for any number of factors:

- Time constraints
- Not having the right skilled team with adequate resources
- A risk averse climate

- Fuzzy goals and lack of direction for the innovation initiative (e.g., scope, what's in, what's outside the box, line/product extensions to what is currently being worked on, etc.)
- Not having a well-defined and clear handoff with a distinct break between concept development and implementation

Falling into Trap #2 can be quite demoralizing and self-defeating if you fall short of meeting the creative productivity goals. Both traps are just that, traps.

DISTRACTIONS FROM CREATIVE WORK

The willingness to experiment with change may be the most essential ingredient to success at anything.

— Pat Summit, lengendary head coach and winner of
8 NCAA woman's college basketball championships

Extreme Time Pressures and Unrealistic Expectations for Creative Productivity are real workplace resistance factors, no doubt about it. So just for some extra s…s and giggles, let's squeeze in a third layer, namely **Distractions from Creative Work**. It can be easy to get submerged in everyday work and become distracted from creative work. The time factor, work pressures and degree of a risk intolerant climate certainly are big time contributors to becoming distracted. Heck, we've got to get the hamburgers out fast, hot and tasty, which takes up a lot of bandwidth.

Often people don't even think about creative work because they are so focused on everyday work. Sound familiar? Thinking about and acting on creative work is in itself a distraction from everyday work. Add to it the habitual and mind numbing, time wasting escape actions of being addicted to gadgets and smartphones…with so many pressing emails to answer (mostly useless)…and checking electronic messaging boards for updates…wasting valuable time surfing the web…and the list goes on. You get the picture. It's so easy *and also convenient* to become distracted— especially if the time, expectation and risk factors aren't established and addressed adequately. Then we become very busy with our *gotta, gotta do's* and our everyday work. That provides some good cover which further distances us from engaging in creative work. However, being busy with our busyness does not match reaching for the brass ring.

MAKE A TWO-BOARD ADJUSTMENT

Relive it

Reflect on and relive the times in your life when you were: enthusiastic, energetic and fit; playful and wonderfully silly; calm and relaxed; intrinsically motivated and fully immersed in the problem; communicative – wholeheartedly listening and empathizing with people; and setting aggressive timelines and gaining traction. Make your list as you relive those times and heighten your awareness. Transfer that energy to your current challenge by developing some of these conditions.

Extreme Time Pressures, Unrealistic Expectations for Creative Productivity and Distractions from Creative Work will rob us of our most precious asset of time and have a debilitating effect on our creative productivity…if we let them!

And speaking of *A C T I O N,* it's high time to summon *The B e y o n d e r* who firmly believes that patience is a far overrated virtue…

...*MOMENTUM*

Xcelerates best concepts and prototypes to action. He has an unrelenting bias for action, an irrepressible optimistic spirit and generously uses humor (especially his own) and intuition to keep things moving forward proactively. Once his sidekick *Plusser* has strengthened a concept to be a **Best Concept**, it is either *IN* or *OUT* of the funnel—no fuzzy, squishy, grey area in between! It's either advanced to prototype, full implementation or deposited unceremoniously in the brine-filled, sour idea/concept pickle barrel. No time for delay, not now, not ever!

His *Powers* are:

Be Optimistic

- Think positive, be resolute and don't become unnerved or deterred when facing complexity or ambiguity.
- See the big picture and don't get bogged down prematurely in too many details or exact terms.
- Maintain a spirited, optimistic attitude even when facing formidable odds.
- See obstacles and take proactive actions to overcome, go around or barrel through them.

Use Humor and Intuition

- Be playful, joyful and spontaneous with ideas and options.
- Tune into what is right in front of you, make mental leaps and act on your hunches and gut instincts.
- Read between the lines, see relationships between things without having the need for overly conclusive data and information.
- See the humor in things, let your emotions flow to recognize and respond to opposites, surprises and serendipity.

Act on It

- Have an unrelenting bias for action, lean into risk and move forward.
- Launch multiple, simultaneous prototypes.
- Experiment, learn, adapt quickly and allocate resources appropriately.
- Orchestrate events to achieve early wins to catapult momentum.

XCELERATE THE MOMENTUM

If you have the opportunity – not a perfect opportunity –
and you don't take it, you may never have another chance.

— Roger Bannister, first athlete to run a sub-4-minute mile

If you look closely you will see a hint of rose tint in *Momentum's* goggles. He's a tough-minded optimist! How can you have a pessimistic attitude when you must **X**celerate the Momentum? How to harness the power of what's possible if you're thinking, *'Let's not get our hopes up too high. We don't want to be let down'?* Or the favorite hedge of corporate America: "Better to under commit and over deliver." Whoa baby, that's a real zinger; gotta put $2 in the zinger jar for that one." I'll bet you dollars to doughnuts those thoughts never entered the minds of rugged pioneers crossing the Rocky Mountains in covered wagons bound for the California Gold Rush. My goodness, who the heck has time for small, modest actions? There is gold in them there hills!

PLAY TO WIN AND NOT TO LOSE

Play for more than you can afford to lose and you will learn the game.

— Winston Churchill, former Prime Minister of the United Kingdom

Extreme Time Pressures, Unrealistic Expectations for Creative Productivity and Distractions from Creative Work prevent us from engaging in creative work where we have to take action and potentially lose. Taking action could be risky, after all we could fail! Who has the time to look through a *Play not to Lose* lens? Flip it and look through a

Play to Win lens where you take action and test your limits. This mindset *actually reduces* risk because we learn and adjust by taking action. A number of research studies point to the correlation of using positive affirmation to unlock creative potential and take action (Freidman and Forster,

2005; Icekson, Roskes, and Moran, 2014). And my guess is your life experiences are similar. When we think and act optimistically, we employ a *Play to Win* mindset which fosters creativity. On the reverse, we subvert creativity when we think and act pessimistically and employ a *Play not to Win* mindset. It is highly problematic for people who are avoidance motivated.

MAKE A TWO-BOARD ADJUSTMENT

Use Creative Affirmations to see your Desired Future

Take these steps:

1. Affirm that you can solve this issue and everything you need to solve it is in your brain right now.
2. Affirm it is important enough to work on and requires creative ideas.
3. Choose a time and a relaxing location that is free from distractions.
4. Transport yourself to the future one year from today and write down the date. You have successfully solved your issue. Take some time to see it!
5. Identify the actions you took this past year to achieve your vision.

Reflect on what occurred and write down the actions you took. Answer the following questions:

1. What did you create?
2. How wide was the gap between where you started and today?
3. Why was it so important to you to go on this journey?
4. What were you most surprised about, and what didn't you expect?
5. What barriers did you encounter?
6. What were the key milestones?
7. How does it feel to have made this successful journey?
8. Where do you go from here?

OPTIMISM AND PESSIMISM, OF TWO HEMISPHERES

The man who is a pessimist before 48 knows too much;
if he's an optimist after it, he knows too little.

— Mark Twain, American author and humorist

Research from disciplines including neurology, physiology, psychiatry and psychology suggest that one component of healthy thinking is contingent on the interconnectedness between the right and left cerebral hemispheres of the brain (Hect, 2013). The mental attitudes of optimism and pessimism are connected with discrete physiological processes between both hemispheres. The right hemisphere plays a predominant role in mediating pessimistic thinking, whereas optimistic thinking is largely mediated by the left hemisphere. Following are four categories to explore:

1. Selective Bias
2. The Optimism Bias
3. Locus of Control
4. Interpreting Events

SELECTIVE BIAS

Most people generally have a distinct, selective bias in what they choose to pay attention to in their environment. One notable exception to this was Sergeant Schultz from the 1960s TV comedy, *Hogan's Heroes*, where he typically pleaded ignorance, even when he knew the POWs were planning some big mischief. He would famously say, "I see nothing! I hear nothing! I know nothing!" He had a neutral *tune out* selective bias.

A person with a pessimistic selective bias (a pessimist) has a thinking style where they see negative things, adverse aspects and conditions of the world. *Ah yes, their glass is half empty.* A pessimist doesn't think the world is made up of limitless opportunities; in fact it's just the opposite. They often zero in on the negative signals and selectively filter out or dismiss the positive cues from a situation. When brainstorming, a person with a pessimistic selective bias might say, "How could it be such a good idea if I came up with it?" "If it is such a good idea, somebody else would have already come up with it." **The Vice** may be teaming up with **The 3 Headed Gremlin** on this one.

On the flipside, a person with an optimistic selective bias (an optimist) has a thinking style where they see many good things and are generally hopeful and confident of what the future holds. *Ah yes, their glass is half full.* From their frame, the world is made up of opportunities. They zero in on the positive and reaffirming signals from their environment, and selectively filter out or dismiss the cues that don't align with and support their sunnier outlook. In the movie, *Field of Dreams,* the lead character Ray walked through his Iowa farmland and heard a voice telling him, "If you build it, he will come." He proceeded and built a baseball diamond on his cornfield and the ghosts of great players of the past, led by the infamous Shoeless Joe Jackson, emerged from the corn field to play ball. That certainly took a damn strong dose of an optimistic selective bias.

THE OPTIMISM BIAS

Optimism with some experience behind it is much more energizing than plain old experience with a certain degree of cynicism.

— Twyla Tharp, dancer and choreographer

Unchecked optimism can get you into trouble (my optimism made me do it). Dr. Tali Sharot (2011), associate professor of cognitive neuroscience at University College London, defines the optimism bias as "the delta between a person's expectation of a future event and the result that actually occurs." If the expectation exceeds actual results, the bias is optimistic. If actual results exceed expected results, the bias is pessimistic. The data is in and tells us that both optimists and pessimists tend to exhibit a stubborn inclination to predict future events accurately. Optimists generally overestimate the probability of achieving positive results and underestimate the probability of realizing negative results. They anticipate living healthier and longer lives, making more money, staying happily married and the list goes on. The human condition strikes again!

You may ask, why do some people have a propensity for the optimism bias? After all, we are highly adaptive and reflective mammals. We learn, have rich life experiences and the scar tissue to prove it. We have experienced reality with the many disconnects that have occurred between anticipated results and actual results. You'd think we would learn to recalibrate our expectations when confronted with disconfirming information and adjust to a formula that more accurately anticipates results. Dr. Sharot reports:

An optimism bias is maintained in the face of disconfirming evidence because optimists update their beliefs more in response to positive information about the future than to negative information about the future.

Fancy that! It's good to have an optimistic bias, and it's smart to turn down the rose tint in those glasses a couple of shades to see reality clearer. Pay attention optimists, *pessimists tend to do just the opposite.* They update their beliefs more accurately when faced with negative information about the future. As you read this, the *'I didn't want to tell you so, but I told you so'* pragmatists are doing a spirited victory jig with a gallon jug of hard cider in one hand and a handful of doughnuts in the other. This risk here for optimists is they reduce their ability to change and adapt when they selectively and often incorrectly update their beliefs in response to positive information. Could a blend possibly be in order here? What if we practice taking a generally optimistic view of a situation, zero in on the power of possible—and also identify where the potential quicksand is so we don't get sucked into it. It's mighty difficult to get out of quicksand when you're in it—unless you have some *me-Tarzan* skills.

LOCUS OF CONTROL

A third distinction between optimists and pessimists is their *locus of control,* or *self-efficacy*, which deals with a person's belief in their ability or inability to control or influence important facets of their life. Albert Bandura (1986) a pioneering social scientist scholar at Stanford University, has written extensively on many social cognitive theories including self-efficacy, which he defines as *"an expectancy or belief of how competently one will be able to enact a behavior in a particular situation."* Optimists generally have a positive self-efficacy, and consequently believe they are capable of performing at certain levels. They have an internal locus of control (their lives are influenced and controlled internally) and trust their ability to influence their environment and social relationships. As a result, they set aggressive goals, pursue positive outcomes, expect to achieve results and strive for success. They engage in situations and don't avoid them (non-avoidance motivation), most often don't view potential barriers as threats and are able to channel anxiety into positive energy.

Conversely, a pessimist has an external locus of control, often thinking their lives are controlled by outside forces. Success and achievement are linked mainly with luck or connections with powerful people or organizations.

They have an inclination to think in terms of potential dangers, threats, worst possible outcomes and aren't likely to be overly hopeful about the future. They can be passive when facing a challenge, believing the probability of succeeding based on their own efforts and actions are moderate. They engage in efforts to avoid failure and potential threats (avoidance motivation) to shield themselves from negative outcomes, losses or increased levels of anxiety.

INTERPRETING EVENTS

A fourth difference between optimists and pessimists is how they interpret events (attribution style) in their lives. They interpret them differently, which impacts their general attitude towards the world. There is some overlap between interpreting events and locus of control. Pessimists attribute unsuccessful outcomes to factors frequently beyond their control and have self-talk like, *"I am generally not competent and frequently fail in many things I attempt to do."* And even when they do achieve successful outcomes, they can interpret the outcome as temporary and unrepeatable: "I *was lucky this time…it won't necessarily happen again*." This way of thinking does not generate positive feelings and does not reinforce confidence about future undertakings. Having lower expectations leads to poorer performance, reduces the positive reinforcement of a success and becomes self-fulfilling as the cycle repeats itself.

Conversely, optimists attribute unsuccessful outcomes to factors that are temporary and isolated. They ascribe success to internal and stable factors. Their self-talk sounds like, "I am quite capable of succeeding in most everything I put my effort into." And if they aren't successful, they have reaffirming self-talk, such as, "This situation was very difficult, and I wasn't successful with my attempt. I believe with modifications the outcome will be different next time." This way of thinking enhances positive feelings and increases confidence about future endeavors. Self-talk like, "I will be successful next time…I place high expectations on myself" leads to increases in performance and becomes self-fulfilling as the cycle repeats itself.

Switching gears, did someone here order a catapult?

CATAPULT THE ENERGY

If you have zest and enthusiasm you attract zest and enthusiasm. Life does give back in kind. Fill the day with enthusiasm. Give the day all you've got, and it will give you all it's got, which will be plenty. Throw your heart over the fence and the rest will follow.

— Norman Vincent Peale, minister and influential author

THE POWER OF HUMOR

We like to laugh, prefer to be around people that make us laugh, and enjoy getting other people to laugh. Laughing is a lot of fun and is highly contagious. I, for one, like to laugh, and as many people who know me can attest to, very much enjoy my own humor (and if you get something out of it, all the better).

Over the past twenty years I have facilitated hundreds of learning programs in all kinds of venues: on high ropes courses, cycling trails, lakes, resorts, Boy Scout camps, corporate offices, and yes, the local Holiday Inn conference room (yawn). Somewhat independent of the physical environment, I have witnessed time and again that when people are enjoying themselves and having fun they learn better. Their guard is down, they aren't nearly as defensive, they interact and collaborate effectively with other people *and are much more playful*! They generate more novel ideas, idea combinations, actionable concepts and prototypes. Time to shout out loud, "Yahtzee!"

Integrating action, play and fun (e.g., get people up off their fannies) into learning programs, meetings and creative problem-solving sessions increases the likelihood that creativity will spark and catch on. Dr. Stuart Brown, M.D. (2010) has spent his career studying how play improves and joyously changes people's lives. In his book, *Play*, he connects the effects of play with creativity. He explains:

When we engage in play at any age, we are open to possibility and the sparks of new insights. We're able to bend the reality of our ordinary lives and in the process germinate new ideas and ways of being. Creative play takes our minds to places we have never been before, pioneering new paths that the real world can follow, like when Einstein came up with his theory of relativity after imagining himself riding on a streetcar travelling at the speed of light.

Fun, play and humor tend to flow together freely and naturally—most of the time *(I did have one participant ask me once, "Just how much fun can you have in a day?").* My guess is she got a little tired out (not used to moving much), and her shoes might have been one size too small. Get her some ice, keep the swelling down! And as a last resort you can always break out the squirt guns on hot days. Yes, humor, fun and play work quite well with learning, thank you. Why is this?

THE NEUROPHYSIOLOGY OF LAUGHTER

There is nothing in the world so irresistibly contagious as laughter and good humor.

— Charles Dickens, 19th c. author, who created great fictional characters

Gelotology is a branch of science dedicated to the study of the psychological and physiological effects of humor and laughter on the brain and the immune system. Using brain-mapping equipment, neurologists have observed that the entire brain is engaged to fully appreciate a joke and humor. *Essentially, the left hemisphere sets up the joke and the right hemisphere helps the brain get the joke.* The result is happiness and laughter happen naturally. This is different from typical emotional responses as they appear to be relegated to specific areas of the brain, while laughter appears to be generated via circuitry that travels through many regions of the brain (Kaufman, 2013). Dr. William Fry (1994) of Stanford University has published a number of studies on the effect laughter has on physiological processes, often comparing the effects of laughter to physical exercise. He shares, "*I believe we laugh with our whole physical being, which serves to stimulate cardiovascular activity.*"

As such it improves mental functioning, increases production of endorphins, releases tension and decreases stress hormones which enhances creative flexibility (*breaking existing thinking and perceiving patterns*). Engaging many regions of the brain is a good practice to tap into creative potential and laughter appears to help grease these skids. So, let's get a-priming the whole brain and get lots of circuits a-firing!

Robert Provine (2001), professor of neurobiology and psychology at the University of Maryland, focuses on the social aspect of laughter and its relationship to creativity. He reports, "*Laughter occurs when people are comfortable with one another, when they feel open and free. And the more laughter there is within a group, higher levels of bonding occur.*"

When people are comfortable and trusting they are more willing to share their over-the-top ideas and build on those from the group. This doesn't happen in groups where foundational trust and positive group dynamics are lacking. Using humor to *jump spark creativity* helps people to make new, interesting and unique connections.

USE LOGIC OR INTUITION IN DECISION MAKING?

Have the courage to follow your heart and intuition.
Everything else is secondary.

— Steve Jobs, entrepreneur and co-founder of Apple

Let's take a leap from laughter to logic and intuition. Logic defined here as "*a particular way of thinking, especially one that is reasonable and based on good judgment.*" No argument here, sounds logical. If you find yourself pitching your product or service idea to the cold-blooded sharks on *Shark Tank*, it would be highly prudent to ensure your presentation is well organized, fact-based and has solid revenue projections. The sharks are seeking rock solid logic before making an investment decision. Not a good move to base the pitch on intuition, a sparkle in your eye or gut instinct. After all, Mr. Wonderful loves his money far too much for those shenanigans. Okay, but when should you pay attention to it?

Dr. Cyndi Burnett, (2015) formerly an associate professor at the Center for Applied Imagination at Buffalo State College in NY, has researched the role intuition plays in creative problem solving. She defines intuition as, "*The process driven by intention, of trusting and action upon one's knowledge at a particular moment in time, and without the conscious evidence of doing so at that moment in time."*

Other researchers (Kaufman, 2009) have defined intuition as, *"a hunch, a gut instinct, an inkling, an energy, a feeling in your bones, an emotion, a voice whispering in your ear, a premonition, a sixth sense, a suspicion, a notion, an idea, an instinct."* And an alternative description has intuition operating at the unconscious or nonconscious level (Dane, Bear, Pratt & Oldham, 2011). With these conditions, your intuition is signaling you to pay attention to something. You might not be able to put your finger on exactly why, and you aren't sure what triggered it. It isn't necessarily logical however you understand or know something. *You feel it.* And you don't feel compelled to think about it or use reason to discover it further. So, should we use logic or intuition?

BEHIND DOOR #2

Twenty-years ago, I led a team of recruiters and trainers at a leading consumer products company. After screening prospective candidates, we conducted round one of phone interviews. In round two we used a structured interviewing method to elicit examples of past performance results and behaviors as these were the best predictors of future performance. For the candidates still standing, in round three we administered psychological and behaviorally based assessments to winnow the list down to a few best candidates. In round four, we came together as a group and applied a weighted criteria decision grid to rate the candidates. The candidates with the highest scores emerged as the best choices. We used a logical method that was replicated by all recruiters in different geographic locations. And it worked well…*most of the time.*

How come not all the time, you ask? On more than a few occasions I had gut instincts (both positive and negative) about different candidates. The decision grid was telling me one thing (the grid made me do it), but my instincts, emotions and intuition were telling me something different from my logic. What I learned here was *to pay attention to the signals from both logic and intuition* and not rely on just one. This enabled me to peel back another layer of the onion, dig deeper and conduct more focused discovery with the candidate. Yes, in this scenario the logic-intuition scale tipped more towards logic, but not entirely. And by doing so, only occasionally did I have to ask the recruiters, *"Tell me again how this person got through?"*

OF TWO MINDS

It is not the biggest, the brightest or the best that will survive, but those who adapt the quickest.

— Charles Darwin, British evolutionary biologist

In their book, *In Two Minds: Dual Process and Beyond*, Jonathan Evans (2009), professor of cognitive psychology at The University of Plymouth, UK, and Keith Frankish, senior lecturer in philosophy at The Open University, Milton Keynes, UK, argue that *we are of two minds* regarding dual-process theories of human reasoning and rationality. They describe two distinct underlying information processing systems that continually interact with each other to assist us in how we think, perceive and respond. The defining features of the Type 1 process (intuitive) are it does not require working memory and is autonomous. It is an evolutionary system that is associative, automatic, unconscious, parallel and fast. The processes are innate and evolved over time. The defining features of the Type 2 process (reflective) are it requires working memory and mental stimulation. It is rule-based, controlled, conscious, serial and slow. The processes are versatile, learned and responsive.

Many of us have been conditioned to value logical thinking most; it is king. Paying attention to the heart and the gut is soft. Hmmm is that so? Do you remember when you fell in love for the first time? Did you get out a piece of paper and list his/her *'exceeds'* attributes on the left side, '*meets'* in the middle and *'needs improvement'* on the right? If you did, do yourself (and us) a favor and not admit it. Better yet, I'll light a candle for you. Of course you didn't! Your heart, gut and intuition went into overdrive  signaling you big time, with lights-a-flashing and whirling and sirens going off. For the big issues, we first make an emotional, instinctual decision, and then use logic to justify it. So, if it works with the big issues, how about letting it work for the medium ones also?

IT'S IN THERE

Sometimes, what you are looking for is already there.

— Aretha Franklin, the 'Queen of Soul' and the first female artist inducted into the Rock and Roll Hall of Fame

There once was a television commercial for Prego spaghetti sauce where a person would ask whether specific ingredients were in the sauce and would receive the same answer to every question. It went something like this: *'Tomatoes?…In there! Garlic?…In there! Carrots?…In there! Half of Italy?…In there!'* Regardless of what was asked for, it was in that bottle of sauce. And so it is with our natural intuitive and logical abilities. They are in there. Should we use logic or intuition in decision making? The answer is *yes*! Pay attention to what your head, heart and gut are saying to you, and have each one keep an eye on the other. Better yet, sleep with one eye open just in case!

And speaking of unbridled *O P T I M I S M and A C T I O N…*

MAKE A TWO-BOARD ADJUSTMENT

Integrate Exercise into your Daily Routine

Physical exercise builds muscle, conditions the heart and the lungs. It also builds, conditions and influences the brain. The brain can be shaped and modified the way muscle can. The more we exercise it, the stronger it becomes.

BATTLE #5

...MOMENTUM
BREAKS THE GRIP OF
THE VICE

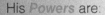

His *Powers* are:

- *Be Optimistic*
- *Use Humor and Intuition*
- *Act on It*

Workload Pressures Resistors

- **Extreme Time Pressures**
- **Unrealistic Expectations for Creative Productivity**
- **Distractions from Creative Work**

TO **X**CELERATE THE MOMENTUM, THE ACTION WE NOW SEE TAKING IS TO LEVERAGE OUR NETWORK...

FIND AND HIRE A TOP BREWMASTER THAT CAN HELP US TO PURCHASE THE EQUIPMENT AND GET INITIAL OPERATIONS SET UP TO HIT THE GROUND RUNNING.

GOT YOU BOTH BEAT, 22 DAYS!

OKAY, OKAY I'M ON BOARD. THE ACTION I NOW SEE TAKING IS DEVELOPING A NEW, CONTEMPORARY, INVITING FOOD MENU THAT WILL ALSO COMPLEMENT THE AMBIANCE OF THE SETTING, AND ATTRACT MANY GUESTS TO OUR NEW LOCATION.

AND I WILL HAVE THIS DONE IN 17 DAYS! I WIN, SEE IF YOU CAN KEEP UP!

THIS IS THE MOST NON FACT BASED CONVERSATION I HAVE EVER HEARD, IT IS BASED SOLELY ON EMOTION, POSITIVITY, AND INTUITION. THIS ISN'T THE TIME FOR ACTION, NOW IS THE TIME TO RETREAT FROM THIS PIPE DREAM.

HECK THE PIED PIPER MADE MORE SENSE.

YOU ARE TOTALLY DISTRACTED AND HAVE BOUGHT INTO THIS CREATIVITY MIRAGE.

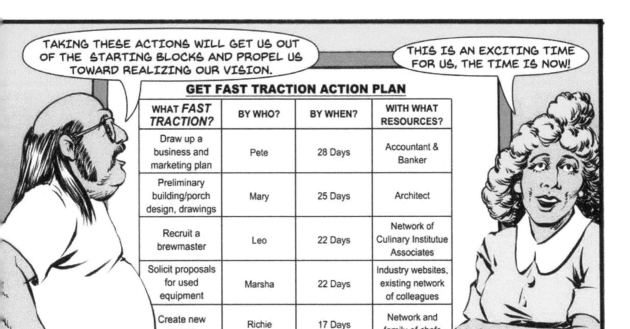

EPISODE PROFILE:
MICHAEL JORDAN

TO SUCCEED, YOU MUST FAIL

I've missed more than 9,000 shots in my career. I've lost almost 300 games. 26 times, I've been trusted to take the game-winning shot and missed. I've failed over and over and over again in my life. And that is why I succeed.

— Michael Jordan, American athlete

Michael Jordan played fifteen seasons in the National Basketball Association (NBA) for the Chicago Bulls and Washington Wizards. The official NBA website states: *"By acclamation, Michael Jordan is the greatest basketball player of all time."* He was one of the most marketed athletes of his generation and was considered instrumental in popularizing the NBA in the 1980s and 1990s.

Source, Google Images

Jordan's individual accomplishments include six NBA Championships and NBA Finals Most Valuable Player Awards; ten All NBA First Team and nine All-Defensive Team designations; fourteen NBA All-Star Game Selections and three All-Star Game MVP Awards, three Steals Titles, and the 1988 NBA Defensive Player of the Year Award. He holds NBA records for highest career regular season scoring average (30.12 points/game) and highest career playoff scoring average (33.45 points/game). He was named the greatest North American athlete of the 20th century by ESPN and was second to Babe Ruth on the Associated Press's list of athletes of the century. Jordan is a two-time inductee into the Naismith Memorial Basketball Hall of Fame, being enshrined in 2009 for his individual career, and in 2010 with the group induction of the 1992 United States men's Olympic basketball team. He became a member of the NBA Hall of Fame in 2015. Although there have been many superstars that have played in the NBA, Michael Jordan is in a league of his own.

MAKE A TWO-BOARD ADJUSTMENT

Pay Attention to and use your Intuition

Put yourself in a position of highest potential. Say you are looking for ways to improve customer service in your business. Go to places where you will experience high levels of customer service (e.g. a five star hotel, a renowned spa). As you experience the service, pay attention to what your heart (emotions) and gut (instincts) are saying to you. Ask, "*What insight am I gaining? What emerges as most important? What is truly unique about this?*"

Tell your subconscious to work on an issue. Write it down on a note pad before going to bed and tell yourself where you want new thinking. When you wake up, write down the ideas you produced. Use this technique throughout the day (less the sleep). Keep your idea capture system with you and write down what your heart and gut tell you. Use spontaneous stimulus to help you to cross-reference new ideas with your existing reservoir of stored information.

IT'S YOUR TIME

In the comic strip *Momentum* used his *Powers* of *Be Optimistic, Use Humor and Intuition* and *Act on It* to **Xcelerate the Momentum, Catapult The Energy** to Break the Grip of **The Vice**. He helped spark the family to use **The Power of Speed** and get their Best Concept/Prototype to action!

See yourself as the anchor leg of a 4x100 meter relay race. Grab the baton and give yourself up to an all-out sprint to the finish line. Summon your full energy, your powerhouse and empty the tank.

There are two kinds of people in this world: talkers and doers. Talkers talk about doing. Doers use their kick to **X**celerate their Best Concept/Prototype to action. *Work out* with **Get Fast Traction; Name, Laugh and Shout at It;** and **Adapt & Adjust** to *Lean into Risk, Embrace Your Dream and Take Proactive Actions to go get it!*

EPISODE III, THE POWER OF SPEED! BATTLE #5

BURST IN HERE WHEN...

You have a Best Concept/Prototype and need to **Xcelerate the Momentum, Catapult it Forward** and implement it.

AND FIGHT OFF THE VICE AND HIS WORKPLACE PRESSURE RESISTORS:

- **Extreme Time Pressures**
- **Expectations for Creative Productivity**
- **Distractions from Creative Work**

POWER SOURCES

- **Best Concept/ Prototype**

...MOMENTUM **VS.** THE VICE

POWERS

- Be Optimistic
- Use Humor and Intuition
- Act on It

KEY ACTIONS

- **Xcelerate the Momentum**
- **Catapult the Energy**

WORKOUTS

- **Get Fast Traction**
- **Name, Laugh and Shout at It**
- **Adapt and Adjust**

OUTCOMES

IMPLEMENTED BEST CONCEPT/ PROTOTYPE

THE POWER OF SPEED

XCELERATE THE MOMENTUM

Burst in here when...you have a Best Concept/Prototype and need to Xcelerate the Momentum, Catapult it Forward and implement it.

ⒹIVERGENT WORKOUT

GET FAST TRACTION

When you **Get Fast Traction**, you diverge and ask who, what, where, when and how questions to develop a Get Fast Traction Action Plan and implement your Best Concept/Prototype. To the fast traction:

Bring forward your Best Concept/Prototype from **Battle #4**:

'My Best Concept/Prototype is...'

- Answer the **Get Fast Traction** who questions: Who needs to support and be enthusiastic about this Best Concept/Prototype? Who do we need assistance from to implement? Who can serve the role of coach? Who are we accountable to and report status? Who has specific expertise to tap into? Who can we pre-test actions plans with? Who needs to make what decisions?

- Answer the **Get Fast Traction** what questions: What are the key tasks to implement the Best Concept/Prototype? What is the best sequencing of the tasks? What tasks are interrelated and contingent upon each other? What are the implementation phases (short, medium, long term)? What decisions need to be made? What resources will be required? What are the consequences of delays? What can go wrong? What would be the likely causes? What are the probabilities? What would be the impact? What is the contingency plan? What are the tripwires that will signal the need to make adjustments?

- Answer the **Get Fast Traction** where questions: Where is the best place to start to implement the Best Concept/Prototype? Where can we gain momentum? Where is the quicksand—difficulty, obstacles, places, events to avoid? Where are special events, times we can connect into?

- Answer the **Get Fast Traction** when questions: When is the best time to start implementing? When do the implementation phases begin and end? When do decisions need to be made? When are the best times to celebrate success?

- Answer the **Get Fast Traction** how questions: How to get early momentum? How to keep energy levels high? How to keep the implementation on schedule and within budget? How to get the buy in, support and resources needed? How to avoid getting sucked into the quicksand? How to celebrate success?

You've identified actions to **Get Fast Traction** and implement your Best Concept/Prototype. Jump spark your implementation within the next 24 hours – at the latest!

Get Fast Traction Action Plan

What Fast Traction?	By Who?	By When?	With What Resources?	What Measures?

ⒹIVERGENT WORKOUT

NAME, LAUGH AND SHOUT AT IT

When you **Name, Laugh and Shout at It** you diverge to defeat the destructive power of the IVOJ and EVOJ. This technique accomplishes two important objectives:

- Acknowledge and illuminate their presence.
- Efficiently dispense and not allow them to sabotage or derail moving forward with your implementation.

When they rear their ugly head, acknowledge their existence, greet and **Name it!** Say, *'"Hello, Yes Butter." I was wondering when you were going to rear your pessimistic head and show up—heck, I expected to hear from you sooner.'*

Now **Laugh at it**. Have a good belly laugh at their expense. Laugh at how ridiculous this pipsqueak twerp of a voice is, in contrast to the power and energy of your Best Concept/Prototype and implementation plan. In comparison, that little squeaky voice is really funny. Go ahead, pull up the laughter from deep in your belly and laugh at them until you have tears in your eyes and your belly hurts. A good minute or two of authentic laughter will do the trick and squash the little half-pint.

After you wipe the tears from your eyes, put the spotlight back on the little twerp and **Shout at it** with your most righteous and indignant voice. Give it a tongue lashing, don't hold back. Give it a loud shout of, "Buona notte," and tell it where to go, where it belongs (your choice of words), out of your consciousness.

Zero in on your implementation plan and **Name** the voice of judgment that may be circling. **Laugh at it** again with a darn good belly laugh. **Shout at It** one more time with a blood-curdling scream!

My Best Concept /Prototype Implementation	The Voice of Judgment

Now that you have silenced the *voice of judgment*, ask, "What additional novel and spicy ideas have I sparked to implement my Best Concept/Prototype?"

THE POWER OF SPEED

CATAPULT THE ENERGY

Burst in here when…you have a **Get Fast Traction Action Plan**, have cleared the path forward and silenced the IVOJ and EVOJ and want to adapt and adjust the plan as needed.

ⒸONVERGENT WORKOUT

ADAPT AND ADJUST

You start with a Get Fast Traction Action Plan, and now it's time to **Adapt and Adjust** the plan as needed. You will develop a performance dashboard with a few gauges and indicators that monitor performance and provide a visual representation of the implementation. You want to be proactive and make any required adjustments early.

Develop performance indicators and an adjusting plan. Your goal is to develop a "vital few" set of gauges and indicators that will provide real time feedback on your progress and signal you if you need to adjust. Use the questions that follow as a guide to develop your dashboard:

- What indicators and gauges to use to measure and report results?
- What are the most critical tasks and processes that must be tracked and measured?
- What measures will tell you how well you're performing?
- What yellow and red flag trip-wire conditions need to occur to trigger action?
- What potential alternative actions do you anticipate having to take?

Real-Time Implementation Dashboard

Indicators	Results	Tripwires	Alternative Actions

Summary of Episode iii, The Power of Speed, Battle #5:

After priming the pump with many tips, tricks, tools, techniques and a comic strip to liberate your *B e y o n d e r Powers*, you sped in with your Best Concept/Prototype, collaborated with *Momentum*, used your *Powers* of *Be Optimistic, Use Humor and Intuition* and *Act on It* to **Get the Momentum** and **Catapult the Energy**. You *worked out* with **Get Fast Traction; Name, Laugh and Shout at It;** and **Adapt and Adjust**. Your outcome is a ready-to-implement Best Concept/Prototype! How sweet it is, Alice!

MAKE A TWO-BOARD ADJUSTMENT

Think and act Efficaciously

Self-efficacy is an expectation, a belief, a trust in yourself that you are competent, and that you are able to perform at high levels. You have confidence in your ability to summon your **Powers**, think and act creatively in situations that require it. To that end:

– Affirm your ability to think and act creatively in situations.
– Actively engage in situations that demand creative thinking. Don't view potential barriers as threats. Channel natural anxiousness into positive action-oriented energy.
– Set aggressive yet achievable goals.
– Measure your results and make real-time adjustments.
– Pursue positive outcomes, expect to achieve results and strive for success.
– Learn by doing, adapt, let go of setbacks and move on.

GET CREATIVITY FIT® APPENDIX

APPENDIX A
UPWARD

ASSESS YOUR *BEYONDER POWERS*

The purpose of this survey is to assess your frequency in using the fifteen *B e y o n d e r Powers* (adapted from Torrance, 1998) and target those to strengthen. For each question rate your frequency in using the *Power* and chart the scores in the Pre-28 Day Challenge Usage Chart. After completing The Challenge re-take the survey and chart the scores in the Post-Challenge Usage Chart. Compare the pre and post survey results and reflect on your accomplishments.

Use the following scale for your answers:

1 = Almost Never 2 = Rarely 3 = Sometimes 4 = Usually 5 = Most Always

When attempting to solve a challenge/problem or pursue an opportunity where novel, valuable and feasible thinking is required, *how frequently do I use the Power…*

Find It
1. Define a variety of challenges, problems or opportunities that could be pursued or solved?

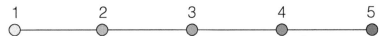

2. Find many problems or opportunities, uncover missing or incomplete information and zero in on the most pertinent facts?

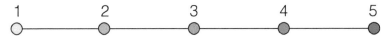

3. Analyze, clarify and reframe various elements of problems and opportunities?

4. Demonstrate genuine curiosity and ask insightful, provocative questions?

See It
5. Fantasize about things that don't yet exist?

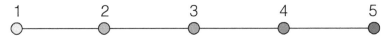

6. Use vivid and varied mental imagery to see the future?

1	2	3	4	5

7. Identify potential barriers that could prevent achieving a future vision?

1	2	3	4	5

8. Draw a sharp distinction between the present and future vision to create a tension that stimulates proactive action?

1	2	3	4	5

Be Versatile
9. Use different approaches to problem-solving?

1	2	3	4	5

10. Simplify problems/opportunities without losing essential details?

1	2	3	4	5

11. View problems/opportunities through various lenses, different frames?

1	2	3	4	5

12. Persevere when facing complex or ambiguous issues and problems?

1	2	3	4	5

Chart the score from questions 1-12 in the Pre-28 Day Challenge Usage Chart. This is how frequently you use your *Black Diamond Powers*!

Be Fluent
13. Generate many ideas for open-ended problems, opportunities and questions?

1	2	3	4	5

14. Use wide and varied stimuli to jump-spark diverse thinking and ideas?

1	2	3	4	5

15. Defer judgment when generating ideas, alternatives and concepts?

| 1 | 2 | 3 | 4 | 5 |

16. Use mechanisms (e.g., idea quotas) to force generating an increased quantity of ideas?

| 1 | 2 | 3 | 4 | 5 |

Be Novel

17. Resist conformity and be independent in thought and action?

| 1 | 2 | 3 | 4 | 5 |

18. Seek originality, break away from obvious, habit-bound and automatic responses?

| 1 | 2 | 3 | 4 | 5 |

19. Strive to generate exaggerated and wild ideas, the wilder the better?

| 1 | 2 | 3 | 4 | 5 |

20. Break down the components/attributes of a problem or opportunity, and generate ideas to improve each component/attribute?

| 1 | 2 | 3 | 4 | 5 |

Stay Open

21. Take adequate time to fully understand the challenge, problem or opportunity, and consider important factors about them?

| 1 | 2 | 3 | 4 | 5 |

22. Think of ideas that are not merely extensions and more of the same?

| 1 | 2 | 3 | 4 | 5 |

23. Keep ideas and options open for as long as possible, and resist the strong knee-jerk temptation to prematurely reach conclusions?

| 1 | 2 | 3 | 4 | 5 |

24. Seek out opposing perspectives, points of view and opinions to gain an appreciative understanding of different or competing alternatives?

1	2	3	4	5

Chart the score from questions 13-24 in the Pre-28 Day Challenge Usage Chart. This is how frequently you use your *Micro-Burst Powers*!

Borrow It
25. Think analogically, borrow ideas from one context and apply them in another?

1	2	3	4	5

26. See a connection from a related problem or idea and repurpose it?

1	2	3	4	5

27. Look laterally for ideas in suitable applications or industries?

1	2	3	4	5

28. Discover how nature goes about solving similar issues?

1	2	3	4	5

Elaborate
29. Expound on ideas by adding enough detail to them, but not excessively.

1	2	3	4	5

30. Develop ideas by improving, embellishing or transforming them.

1	2	3	4	5

31. Frame ideas so they can be understood by other people and aren't perceived to be too complex, costly or far out?

1	2	3	4	5

32. Orchestrate the details of ideas so it is clear what actions should be taken by whom, by when and with what resources?

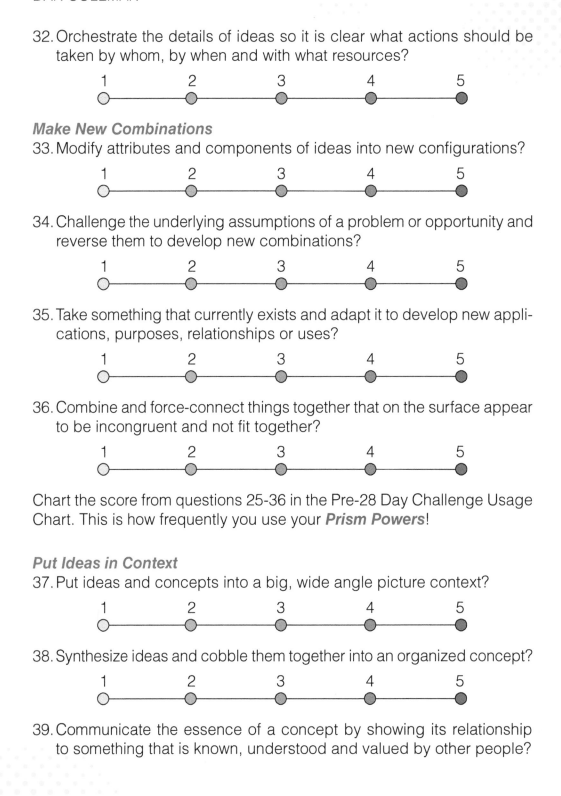

1   2   3   4   5

Make New Combinations

33. Modify attributes and components of ideas into new configurations?

1   2   3   4   5

34. Challenge the underlying assumptions of a problem or opportunity and reverse them to develop new combinations?

1   2   3   4   5

35. Take something that currently exists and adapt it to develop new applications, purposes, relationships or uses?

1   2   3   4   5

36. Combine and force-connect things together that on the surface appear to be incongruent and not fit together?

1   2   3   4   5

Chart the score from questions 25-36 in the Pre-28 Day Challenge Usage Chart. This is how frequently you use your **Prism Powers**!

Put Ideas in Context

37. Put ideas and concepts into a big, wide angle picture context?

1   2   3   4   5

38. Synthesize ideas and cobble them together into an organized concept?

1   2   3   4   5

39. Communicate the essence of a concept by showing its relationship to something that is known, understood and valued by other people?

1   2   3   4   5

40. Quantify the economic value of a concept even if it is difficult to do so?

1   2   3   4   5

Evaluate and Select It

41. Pay attention to what your logic, emotions and intuition say to you?

1   2   3   4   5

42. Think critically and use criteria to help deduce reasonable and sound conclusions?

1   2   3   4   5

43. Compare, contrast and make decisions on the appropriateness, value and difficulty among competing alternatives?

1   2   3   4   5

44. Choose options you believe will realize a solid return and not have a daunting amount of difficulty to implement?

1   2   3   4   5

Strengthen It

45. Identify the plusses and potential of ideas and concepts by first listening for what's right about them?

1   2   3   4   5

46. Use goal wishing ('I wish...') to generate options to overcome the drawbacks of ideas and concepts?

1   2   3   4   5

47. Give ideas and concepts a fair hearing, and don't be impatient and hasty in making premature decisions?

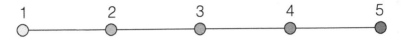

48. Develop problem-prevention actions to minimize the probability and negate the impact of factors that could derail implementing an idea or concept?

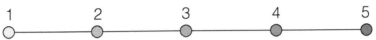

Chart the score from questions 37-48 in the Pre-28 Day Challenge Usage Chart. This is how frequently you use your **Plusser Powers**!

Be Optimistic
49. Think positive, be resolute and don't become unnerved or deterred when facing complexity or ambiguity?

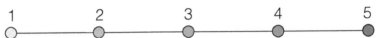

50. See the big picture and don't get bogged down prematurely in too many details or exact terms?

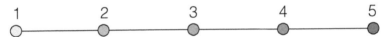

51. Maintain a spirited, optimistic attitude even when facing formidable odds?

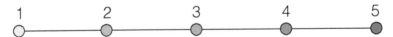

52. See obstacles, and take proactive actions to overcome, go around or barrel through them?

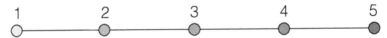

Use Humor and Intuition
53. Be joyful, playful and spontaneous with ideas and options?

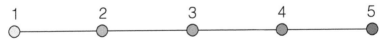

54. Tune into what is right in front of you, make mental leaps and act on your hunches and gut instincts?

1	2	3	4	5

55. Read between the lines, see relationships between things without having the need for overly conclusive data or information?

1	2	3	4	5

56. See the humor in things, let your emotions flow to recognize and respond to opposites, surprises and serendipity?

1	2	3	4	5

Act on It

57. Have an unrelenting bias for action, lean into risk and move forward?

1	2	3	4	5

58. Launch multiple simultaneous prototypes?

1	2	3	4	5

59. Experiment, learn and adapt quickly, and allocate/reallocate resources appropriately?

1	2	3	4	5

60. Orchestrate events to achieve early wins to catapult momentum?

1	2	3	4	5

Chart the score from questions 49-60 in the Pre-28 Day Challenge Usage Chart. This is how frequently you use your *Momentum Powers*!

B E Y O N D E R POWERS

PRE-28 DAY CHALLENGE USAGE CHART

	Black Diamond	Micro-Burst	Prism	Plusser	Momentum
Very High Use >50					
High Use 40-49					
Moderate Use 30-39					
Low Use < 30					

To gain additional insight, please answer the following questions:

- Which *Powers* do you use most frequently and why?

- Which *Powers* do you use least frequently and why?

- Which *Powers* do you feel are your strengths and why?

- Which *Powers* do you feel are your weaknesses and why?

- Which *Powers* when strengthened, do you feel will provide you with the greatest impact? (These could be strengths or weaknesses.)

- Which three *Powers* do you want to target to strengthen?

- *'I will know I have reached my skill development goals when...'*

BEYONDER POWERS

POST-28 DAY CHALLENGE USAGE CHART

Upon completing The Challenge re-take the survey and chart the scores.

	Black Diamond	Micro-Burst	Prism	Plusser	Momentum
Very High Use >50					
High Use 40-49					
Moderate Use 30-39					
Low Use < 30					

To gain additional insight, please answer the following questions:

- What is the difference in your Pre-28 Day Challenge and Post-Challenge scores? What do you attribute these differences to?

- Which *Powers* do you now use most frequently and why?

- Which *Powers* do you feel are your strengths?

- Which *Powers* going forward do you feel will provide you with the greatest impact?

- Did you reach your development goals? Why or why not?

- What adjustments do you need to make going forward?

TAKE A CREATIVE PRODUCTIVITY SNAPSHOT

You've targeted the *Powers* to strengthen and it's time to take a baseline snapshot of your current creative productivity. This snapshot is your starting point, what your current creative productivity is. If you are like most people, this isn't written down because you aren't tracking it. Use the following questions over the next week to establish your baseline creative productivity. Generally speaking, *on a weekly basis...*

- How many problem statements do you generate?

- How many data collection/analysis studies do you conduct?

- How many ideas do you generate?

- Of the ideas you generate, how many are novel and imaginative?

- How many ideas do you make feasible?

- How many concepts (from groups of ideas) do you develop?

- Of the concepts you generate/develop, how many prototypes do you implement?

- Of the prototypes you implement, how many get traction?

CREATIVE PRODUCTIVITY SNAPSHOT

Chart and assess your Pre-28 Day Challenge Creative Productivity and identify your goals. Return in 28 days, chart and assess your Post-Challenge results.

CREATIVE PRODUCTIVITY CATEGORIES	GOALS	PRE-28 DAY CHALLENGE	POST-CHALLENGE
Problem Statements			
Data Collection and Analysis Studies			
Ideas			
Novel Ideas			
Feasible Ideas			
Concepts/ Prototypes and Solutions			
Implemented Prototypes			
Prototypes that Gain Traction			

APPENDIX B
ANCHOR THE CREATIVE AND PHYSICAL EXERCISE HABIT

A FEW POINTS ON POSITIVE HABIT FORMATION

Merriam-Webster defines habit as, "a usual way of behaving, something a person does often in a regular and repeated way." It's automatic; it's something you do that is part of the way you live your life. It isn't something you do occasionally or only at times when you need a big idea!

It may be counterintuitive to think about creativity and habit in the same thought - they appear to be incongruent. Creativity is about novelty and variance and habit is about routine. Creativity is first an attitude about life. What is routine is that creative people routinely think about and respond to challenges in fresh and unique ways. They don't go down the well-worn donkey paths the crowd automatically goes down.

In her wonderful book, *The Creative Habit*, dance choreographer Twila Tharp (2003) wrote about *creativity being augmented by routine and habit*. Over thirty years she created more than 130 dances for her company, the Joffrey Ballet, New York City Ballet, Paris Opera Ballet, London's Royal Ballet and American Ballet Theatre. She reported that *"creativity is a habit and the best creativity is a result of good work habits."* Developing the creative habit is no different than developing any other habit. And like with any habit, creativity can be either encouraged or discouraged. Let's enthusiastically encourage it! Your altitude will be determined by your creative attitude, skills and habits. Following are three principles to employ to quickly accelerate out of the starting blocks:

- THE DRIVING FORCE BEHIND ALL INNOVATION IS CREATIVITY.
- BEHIND CREATIVITY ARE POSITIVE HABITS.
- IF YOU WANT TO SPARK MORE INNOVATION, ANCHOR THE CREATIVE HABIT.

ANCHOR THE CREATIVE AND PHYSICAL EXERCISE HABIT

Thinking creatively is good for the mind, the spirit, the heart and the gut. This is the central theme of this program. You produce more novel and feasible ideas and actions when you proactively think creatively. You can't increase muscular strength by talking about lifting weights; you have to lift weights (what a novel thought). And the same holds true for generating ideas to *Lean into Risk, Embrace Your Dream and Take Proactive Actions to go get it!* You can't just think and talk about it, you have to fully commit to it to get results.

Why Integrate Creative Thinking and Physical Exercise?

I'm so glad you asked. *Flashback:* About two decades ago, I began facilitating creative thinking programs for groups using somewhat *non-traditional, kinesthetic learning methods* including ropes courses, cycling, hiking and orienteering. With these methods, learning takes place via the group being engaged in experiential, physical activities versus listening to lectures or watching demonstrations.

I designed the programs so the group experienced the kinesthetic learning in the morning of day one. The *classroom instruction* segment would follow in the afternoon. The idea was to use the natural *energy* created from the kinesthetic experience and use it to help fuel the classroom instruction. After all, people were high fiving each other on the ropes course, seeing how fast they could race on the bikes and compete on the orienteering course to complete it first. Funny thing happened on the way to the classroom segment – the energy didn't entirely transfer over (especially with the two-day programs). I would ask the group, *"Are you the same people I saw high fiving on the ropes course this morning? You certainly resemble them, but you aren't acting like them now. Where's the same energy?"* Newsflash: the program design was flawed.

Fast forward to today where the programs are designed so the kinesthetic experience and the *classroom instruction* are integrated. For example, on a four stage cycling event the group:

- Prioritizes the problem statements to work on in advance of the kinesthetic experience.
- Uses **Divergent and Convergent Workouts** and takes full advantage of the contributing endorphins and generates novel ideas to solve the problem statements; prioritizes the most feasible ideas; organizes the ideas into an actionable concept/prototype; and strengthens the concept/prototype to be a Best Concept/Prototype.
- By integrating the creative thinking with the physical exercise, the group achieves very impressive results virtually every time – **Boom**!

Physical Exercise and Brain Connection

Over the past twenty-five years the progress in brain neuroscience research has been extraordinary. Physical exercise is good for the body; it builds muscle and conditions the heart and the lungs. It also builds, conditions and influences the brain. The brain is an adaptable organ that can be shaped similarly to the way muscles can be strengthened. The more we exercise the stronger and more versatile the brain becomes.

In his national bestseller, *Spark*, John Ratey (2008) wrote about the science of exercise and the brain. At a base point he outlined that when we get our blood pumping, we elevate endorphins, hormones produced in the body and the brain that serve as natural morphine. They are released when the body and the brain are being taxed. Exercise also increases levels of serotonin, norepinephrine and dopamine, important neurotransmitters that impact our thinking and emotions. Exercise improves our ability to learn on three fundamental levels:

- It sharpens our mindset to improve alertness, attention and motivation.
- It readies and primes nerve cells to communicate and bind to one another at a cellular level, which helps us to take in new information.

- It sparks the development of new nerve cells from stem cells in the hippocampus region of the brain (responsible for collecting incoming stimuli, cross referencing the new information with stored information and forwards it to the prefrontal cortex for processing).

The Impact of Physical Exercise on Convergent and Divergent Thinking

A research team from Leiden University in the Netherlands (Colzato, L., Szapora, A., Pannekoek, J., Hommel, B., 2013) investigated whether creativity in divergent and convergent thinking tasks was impacted by moderate and intense physical exercise in athletes and non-athletes. Ninety-six healthy, native Dutch participants (48 females, 48 males), of which 48 were athletes and 48 non-athletes participated in the study. Participants were considered athletes if they exercised at least three times a week during the recent two years and non-athletes if they did not exercise on a regular basis (less than once per week).

Creative Thinking Tasks

The divergent thinking task used was *alternate uses* where participants were asked to list as many possible uses for six common household items (e.g. pen, towel, bottle). The convergent thinking task used was *remote association* where participants were presented with three unrelated words (e.g., time, hair, stretch) and asked to find a common associate (e.g. long). In the study four scores were considered:

- *Flexibility:* The number of different categories used.
- *Originality:* Each response is compared to the total number of responses from all of the participants. Responses given by only 5% of the group count as unusual (1 point) and responses given by only 1% of the group count as unique (2 points).
- *Fluency:* The total of all responses.

- *Elaboration:* The amount of detail (e.g., "a door stop" counts 0, whereas "a door stop to prevent a door slamming shut in a strong wind" counts 2 (1 point for explanation of door slamming and another for further detail about the wind).

Method

All participants were tested individually. Half the participants in each group executed the creativity tasks during stationary bike cycling, the other half after the cycling. During the moderate cycling condition, participants cycled at a normal pace without exhausting themselves. During the intense cycling condition, the participants cycled at a maximum level of effort. Participants were provided with a printed version of the creativity tasks on a clipboard positioned in front of them on the cycle ergometer so they could fill in their responses comfortably while cycling. Other possible moderating factors were taken into account such as the intensity of the exercise (which was moderate or high in different sessions) and the overlap between the exercise and the creativity task (with the latter performed during or after exercise).

Results

The results provided preliminary evidence that exercise may enhance convergent thinking in individuals with a higher degree of physical fitness as athletes benefited from the exercise in the convergent thinking task. However, non-athletes did not benefit from exercise. It caused their performance to drop in both creativity tasks. The research team speculated that exercise may lead to 'ego-depletion' (decision-making process in your brain when you are going against your preferences) and you exhaust limited cognitive-control resources that are then no longer available for the control of processes involved in convergent and divergent thinking. Because athletes tended to benefit from the exercise in the convergent-thinking task, they speculated that athletes are shielded from the exercise-induced cognitive costs that non-athletes exhibited.

Give Your Ideas Some Legs
The Positive Effect of Walking on Creative Thinking

Stanford University researchers Marily Oppezzo and Daniel Schwartz (2014) conducted four experiments to measure the effects that walking has on creative thinking. 48 undergraduate psychology students from a community college and a private university participated in the study. They found that walking boosts both divergent and convergent thinking skills in real time and shortly thereafter. The majority of participants benefited most from walking versus sitting with a 60 percent average increase in creative productivity. Additionally, walking outside produced the most novel and highest quality analogies, opening up the free flow of ideas. Following are descriptions of the four experiments:

Creative Thinking Tasks

The divergent thinking task used was *alternate uses* where participants were asked to list as many possible uses for common household items (e.g., pen, towel, bottle). The convergent thinking task used was *remote associations* where participants were presented with three unrelated words (e.g., time, hair, stretch) and asked to find a common associate (e.g., long).

Experiment #1:

Participants completed the divergent task first when sitting and then when walking on a treadmill. They also completed the convergent task first by sitting and then walking on a treadmill. Walking had a large effect on creativity as most of the participants benefited from walking compared with sitting. When walking, participants talked more and generated more novel and appropriate uses. 81% of the participants improved their performance on the divergent task. 23% of the participants improved their performance on the convergent task.

Experiment #2:

Participants completed the divergent task when seated and then walking, when walking and then seated, or when seated twice. Walking led to higher scores on the divergent thinking task. On the 1st round, participants who walked did better than those who sat, and those who only sat did not improve across the rounds. After the participants walked, there was a positive residue effect when participants subsequently sat; their creativity was higher than those who had not walked.

Experiment #3:

The procedure differed from Experiment #2 in two ways: 1st, participants walked outside along a path through a university campus. 2nd, after doing the first divergent task, those in the sit condition moved to a different indoor room. Those in the walk-walk condition took a brief break before continuing on the outdoor path. As in Study #2, walking led to improved creative performance on the divergent thinking task and had a positive residue effect when participants subsequently sat. The effect of being outdoors was inconclusive.

Experiment #4:

This experiment introduced two major changes: (1) It employed a different measure of creativity, the generation of analogies; (2) It separated walking from moving through an outdoor space. Participants sat inside, walked on a treadmill inside, walked outside or were rolled outside in a wheelchair. Of those who walked, 95% generated at least one novel high-quality analogy compared with 50% of those who sat. The effects of outdoor stimulation and walking were separable. Both walking and being outdoors independently increased novelty. Walking appears to prompt high structure and novelty, whereas the outdoors seems to influence novelty. Walking opens up a free flow of ideas and is a simple solution to the goals of increasing creativity and increasing physical activity.

Conclusion:

Walking substantially enhanced creativity by two different measures: For the three divergent task experiments, 81%, 88% and 100% of participants were more creative walking than sitting. For the analogy task study, 100% of participants who walked outside generated at least one novel, high-quality analogy compared with 50% of those seated inside. Walking worked indoors on a treadmill and outdoors at a bustling university.

Embrace the Dream and Exercise While you do it

Over the past decade, I've coached north of a few hundred people and helped them to identify, embrace and develop a high level plan to chase their personal dream. Most times we integrated the use of creative thinking tools and workouts and some form of physical exercise into the personalized method. The good news is that, almost universally, people reported they were able to focus in on their dream, embrace it and put together a plan to go after it. Also, greater than 75% of the people reported they found physical exercise to have been a positive stimulus in generating ideas and actions. Additionally, 67% of the people reported using the creative thinking tools and workouts (with a little prodding from the creativity coach) over the course of the coaching sessions. The results of my field based application were similar with the results of the previously cited academic experiments. Onward & Upward!

The Romans taught their children that nothing was to be learned sitting.

—Seneca, Roman philosopher

Areas of Physical Fitness

Experts from the United States Department of Health and Human Services (2018) report that overall physical fitness is made up of five conditioning areas. Each area has an optimal measure of fitness, and when combined together with the other areas provide an overall benchmark of physical fitness.

Cardio-Respiratory Fitness: The body's ability to perform large-muscle, whole-body exercise at moderate to vigorous intensities that force the cardiovascular system (lungs, heart, blood vessels) to exert for extended periods of time.

Musculoskeletal Fitness: The integrated function of muscle strength, muscle endurance and muscle power to enable performance of work.

Flexibility: The range of motion available at a joint or group of joints to move freely.

Balance: The ability to maintain equilibrium while moving or while stationary.

Speed: The ability to move the body quickly.

The American College of Sports Medicine (ACSM) is the largest sports medicine and exercise science organization in the world and is dedicated to advancing scientific research to provide educational and practical applications of exercise science and sports medicine. ACSM (2016) reports that for gains in fitness *the magic ingredient is variety*. If you do the same routines over and over the body will plateau in muscular strength and cardiovascular fitness. When do you know it's time to switch it up? Pay attention to and listen to your body—it requires new stimulus. *Periodization* is a training method that incorporates changes in training intensity and volume to secure fitness and strength gains. The changes don't have to be big (e.g., modify the number of sets/reps, add more weight to the bar/machine or rest for varying time intervals between sets). If you are used to resistance training, switch it up and play some handball, squash or go skiing. If you are bored with your workouts, if they are too easy or if your results have plateaued, shake it up and make some changes!

Physical Exercise Intensity

Health professionals from the Mayo Clinic Healthy Living Program (Sood, 2013) outline two fundamental ways to measure physical exercise intensity:

- *How you feel when exercising*: A subjective measure of how hard the exercise feels to you when you are doing it—your perceived level of exertion.
- *Your heart rate*: A more objective measure of physical exercise intensity. During physical exercise the higher your heart rate, the higher the intensity.

You can use either measure. A heart rate monitor will measure it more precisely. If you are in sync with your body during workouts, you may be fine without the monitor as you are in tune with your intensity level.

To gauge physical exercise intensity determine your maximum heart rate, which is the upper limit of what your cardiovascular system can manage during physical exercise (the number of times your heart should beat per minute). For moderate intensity exercise the Mayo Clinic recommends a heart rate of 65 to 75 percent of your maximum heart rate. To determine this number, subtract your age from 220 and apply the percentages to it. For example, if you are 40 years old, your maximum target heart rate is 180 beats per minute. Multiply it by 65 to 75 percent and your range is between 117 and 135 beats per minute. If you are just beginning an exercise program or not fit, it's best to zero in on the lower end. If you are fit, aim at the higher end. Let's go!

- If you currently have a physical exercise regimen, continue to use it.
- If you previously had a physical exercise regimen but have gotten away from it, resurrect and re-implement it.
- If you aren't currently engaged in physical exercise workouts, get started (e.g., go for walks at a brisk clip to get your heart rate elevated).
- Over the next 48 hours, chart your physical exercise regimen. There are many resources available to develop your plan (e.g. Body for Life, Yoga with Adriene and The P90 X Workout Schedule to name

just a few). Talk with other people who are active or to a fitness coach for ideas. Don't complicate it, just develop your plan. The secret sauce is to **take action**!

The idea is to develop and implement an integrated workout regimen to leverage the positive benefits of physical exercise (when the endorphins are elevated, you are primed and ready) and use it to fuel your creative thinking efforts:

- Precede the physical exercise workout with a stretching/warm-up routine to focus on the creative thinking challenge. Spend five minutes and focus in on the area where you want novel, actionable thinking.
- Engage in a minimum thirty minute physical exercise workout to get your heart rate elevated. During the physical workout you can use **Divergent and Convergent Workouts** to spark your thinking, or just pay attention and make mental notes of the problems/ideas/options that are sparked and jump into your mind.
- After the workout immediately capture what you generated via your idea capture system – (e.g., post-it notes, iPhone, notepad, etc.).
- Take some action on what you produced within 24 hours.

Good things happen when you hustle, when you develop and adopt a regimen. And speaking of that the time has come, the time is now. Map out your plan to:

- Train your Technique and Strengthen Your *Powers*!
- Anchor the *Creative & Physical Exercise Habit*!
- Increase your innovation productivity.
- *Lean into Risk, Embrace Your Dream and Take Proactive Actions to go get it*!

To develop your plan, use the output/information from:

- The tips, tricks, tools, techniques, **Divergent and Convergent Workouts** and Two-Board Adjustments in **Episodes i, ii** and **iii.**
- The weekly and 28-day planning, assessing and reflecting questions.

MY 28 DAY CREATIVE & PHYSICAL EXERCISE PLAN

Week One

Framework	Goals	Workouts

Creative Thinking

- problem statements

- ideas

- concepts/prototypes

- implementation actions

Physical Exercise

- cardiorespiratory

- strength

- flexibility

Results and adjustments for next week:

Week Two

Framework	Goals	Workouts

Creative Thinking

- problem statements

- ideas

- concepts/prototypes

- implementation actions

Physical Exercise

- cardiorespiratory

- strength

- flexibility

Results and adjustments for next week:

Week Three

Framework	Goals	Workouts

Creative Thinking

- problem statements

- ideas

- concepts/prototypes

- implementation actions

Physical Exercise

- cardiorespiratory

- strength

- flexibility

Results and adjustments for next week:

Week Four

Framework	Goals	Workouts

Creative Thinking

- problem statements

- ideas

- concepts/prototypes

- implementation actions

Physical Exercise

- cardiorespiratory

- strength

- flexibility

Results and adjustments for next week:

WEEKLY PLANNING, ASSESSMENT AND REFLECTION GOAL-TENDING QUESTIONS

Creative Thinking

- What are my goals to strengthen my creative thinking **Powers**?

- Which tips, tricks, tools techniques, **Divergent and Convergent Workouts** and Two-Board Adjustments to implement/*work out* with?

- What are my results and key insights?

- What adjustments to make for next week?

Physical Exercise

- What are my goals for physical exercise?

- What exercises/techniques/regimen to use/implement?

- What are my results and key insights?

- What adjustments to make for next week?

MAKE A TWO-BOARD ADJUSTMENT

Less is More to Start With

A small habit is easier to maintain than a big one. Start with a shorter time frame—say 20 minutes a day, and then increase it to 30 - 45 minutes a day once you've established the cadence. Keep your schedule consistent and sustainable so it becomes part of your life. Tie it to another ritual that is already hardwired into your schedule.

A FEW FINAL THOUGHTS

Well there you have it. You worked through **Episodes i, ii** and **iii** and **Battles 1-5**. It took attitude, smarts, energy, persistence and calcium in the backbone! Along the journey you adopted a discipline and cadence. You made the concerted effort and put in the hard work. You:

- Trained your technique and strengthened your *Powers*.
- Anchored the Creative and Physical Exercise (bonus) Habits.
- Increased your innovation productivity.
- *Leaned into Risk, Embraced Your Dream and Took Proactive Actions to go get it!*

I congratulate you and I think it is great. More important, I bet you do too!

REDISCOVER

My logical and intuitive guess is you knew all along what was involved in this program. You rediscovered what you already knew. You have the capability, the creative fire power to navigate through the whitewater rapids of thinking, perceiving and acting more creatively. *The B e y o n d e r s will always be with you.* The challenge is to continue to liberate their *Powers… tap into and hunt the good stuff that's already in there…Get it out…and Xcelerate it to full power and action*!

I hope you enjoyed this journey at least half as much as I did in developing it. The principles are timeless: *Set challenging goals and go after them; forge a tough-minded optimistic attitude; train your technique; learn, adapt and move forward enthusiastically.* We learn nothing when standing at the summit. We learn everything during our preparation, conditioning, practice regimen, ascent and descent.

I trust you still share in my tough-minded optimism that it is **Your Time** to re-energize and continue the journey…to live an adventurous, fulfilling and inspiring life…*to Lean into Risk, Embrace Your Dream and Take Proactive Action to go get it.* And yes…to become the person you have always been capable of becoming!

With Energy,
Dan

MAKE A TWO-BOARD ADJUSTMENT

Developing Habits Means Doing

In an iconic speech, "Citizenship in a Republic," also known as "Man in the Arena" (Morris, 2010), delivered at the Sorbonne in Paris, France on April 23, 1910, President Theodore Roosevelt thundered:

"It is not the critic who counts; not the person who points out how the strong man stumbles, or where the doer of deeds could have done better.

The credit belongs to the man who is actually in the arena, whose face is marred by dust and sweat and blood; who strives valiantly; who spends himself in a worthy cause; who at the best knows in the end triumph of high achievement, and who at the worst, if he fails, at least fails while daring greatly, so that his place shall never be with those cold and timid souls who know neither victory nor defeat."

AN INVITATION

While the 28 Day Challenge comes to a close, the ascent up the creative thinking skill ladder continues - the climb is where the real action is. Yes, the learning, growth, skill mastery and exhilaration takes place during the journey.

When you get a few free minutes, drop me a note and let me know how your journey up the creative thinking skill ladder is progressing. I'm interested in learning about what you have adapted/developed to strengthen your **Powers**. Achieving skill mastery takes time...and taking time to share and teach good practices shortens the time...the ascent. I look forward to hearing from you. Thank you in advance.

Dan Coleman

DAN COLEMAN

Dan Coleman, the founder of Excelsior Learning, is consistently praised by his clients as a knowledgeable and energizing speaker and trainer who brings fresh content, practical tools and unique experiential learning methods to deliver training that sticks. Prior to founding Excelsior Learning, Dan led national account sales and negotiation teams at AT&T and American Greetings and was a senior manager with Accenture. He is a leading authority on how to use creative thinking tools and practices to strengthen creative thinking and negotiation skills. Over the past two decades, Dan has trained thousands of people in his nontraditional, custom-designed programs.

Speaking & Training Topics:

Get Creativity Fit® and Jump Spark more Innovation is a fast-paced, hands on program (in-person or virtual) designed to foster novel thinking and taking action **NOW**! In this program you meet **The Beyonders** who use their **Powers** to conquer *The Resistors* who try to block novel thinking and taking action. By *working out* with powerful *Divergent and Convergent Thinking Workouts*, you encounter immediate learning, and generate novel and feasible ideas to solve individual or team challenges.

Anchor Negotiations @ Aspiration Point…or Nothing is a hands-on, energizing program (in-person or virtual) designed to accelerate the use of a potent mix of *Collaborative, Competitive*, and *People-Centered Negotiation Strategies*. Post-program, you engage in a 21 Day Challenge to anchor the use of strategies as a repeatable habit.

Dan has a B.S. from State University of New York at Plattsburgh and has completed course work towards an M.A. in Creative Studies at the Center for Applied Imagination at Buffalo State College, NY.

DAN COLEMAN

Dan can be reached at:

330.284.5446
dancoleman@excelsior-learning.com
www.excelsior-learning.com
https://www.linkedin.com/in/dan-coleman-1607b01;

Representative Clients:

- ADS
- American Greetings
- Applied Industrial Technologies
- Asurion
- Diebold Nixdorf
- FEDEX Custom Critical
- GOJO Industries
- Landmark Plastics
- Main Street Gourmet
- Mitsubishi Power

- Moen
- MTD
- Praxair
- P&G
- Progress Lighting
- Rinnai America
- ShurTech Brands
- Swagelok
- Therma Tru
- Thermo Fisher Scientific

Another Book by Dan Coleman

Bursts of Fresh-Squeezed Ideas

A Program To Ignite Your
Creative-Thinking Skills

REFERENCES

Adams, D. (2017). Digital Trends. The Best of Biomimicry.

Albert Einstein. (n.d.). AZQuotes.com. Retrieved February 16, 2020, from AAZQuotes.com Web site: https://www.azquotes.com/quote/455371

Allen, D. (2015). Getting Things Done. New York, NY: Penguin Books.

Amabile, T. M. (1996). Creativity in Context. Boulder, CO: Westview Press.

Amabile, T. (2002). Time Pressure and Creativity: Why Time is Not on Your Side. Harvard Business School Working Knowledge, July 19, 2002.

Amabile, T. M. (2012). Componential Theory of Creativity Working Paper 12-096. Harvard Business School.

American College of Sports Medicine (1998): Position Stand 'The recommended Quantity and Quality of Exercise for Developing and Maintaining Cardiorespiratory and Muscular Fitness and Flexibility in Healthy Adults.' Medicine and Science in Sports and Exercise. 30:975-991.

Bandura, A. (1986). Social Foundations of Thought & Action. Englewood Cliffs, NJ: Prentice-Hall.

Biography.com editors (2020). Harriet Tubman Biography. Biography.com website.

Brown, T. (2010). Play. How it Shapes the Brain, Opens the Imagination, and Invigorates the Soul. Penguin Books.

Burkus, D. & Oster, (2012). Noncommissioned work: Exploring the influence of structured free time on creativity and innovation. *Journal of Strategic Leadership*, 4(1), 48-60.

Burnett, C. (2015). Exploring the Role of Intuition in Creative Problem Solving. The International Journal of Creativity and Problem Solving.

Buzan, T. (2005). The ultimate book of mind maps: Unlock your creativity boost your memory change your life. London: Thorsons.

Calarco, A. & Gurvis, J. (2006). Center for Creative Leadership Publications.

Carson, R. (1965). *The Sense of Wonder*. New York, NY: Harper & Row.

Carson, R. (2003). Taming Your Gremlin. New York, NY: Harper Collins.

Carson, S. (2010). Your Creative Brain. San Francisco, CA: Jossey-Bass.

Cialdini, R. (2009). Influence. The Psychology of Influence. Harper Collins.

Coleman, D. (2008). Bursts of Fresh-Squeezed Ideas. Dewittville, NY: Chautauqua Press.

Colzato, L., Szapora, A., Pannekoek, J. N., & Hommel, B. (2013). The impact of physical exercise on convergent and divergent thinking. *Frontiers in human neuroscience*, 7, 824. https://doi.org/10.3389/fnhum.2013.00824

Covey, S. (1990). Fireside, (1990). New York, NY.

Coyle, D. (2010). The Talent Code. Arrow Books.

Coyle, D. (2012). The Little Book of Talent. New York, NY: Bantam Books.

Csikszentmihalyi, M. (1990). Flow: The psychology of optimal experience. New York, NY: Harper & Row.

Dane E., Baier, M., Pratt, M. & Oldham, G. (2011). Rational Versus Intuitive Problem Solving. How Thinking off the Beaten Path can Stimulate Creativity. Psychology of Aesthetics, Creativity and the Arts.

Davis, G. (2004). Creativity is Forever. Dubuque, IA: Kendall/Hunt.

De Bono, E. (1982). Lateral thinking for management. London: Penguin Books.

Duhigg, C. (2014). The Power of Habit. New York, NY: Random House.

Dworkin, M. (1959. Dewey on Education, Selections. Library of Congress Catalog Card Number 59-15893.

Dyer, F. (2010). Edison: His Life and Inventions. FQ Books.

Eberle, R. F. (1972). Scamper: Games for Imagination development: Buffalo, NY: DOK.

Eblin, Scott. "5 Simple Ways to Make Creative Thinking a Daily Habit." *Govexec. com*, 28 May 2015.

Einstein, Albert. (n.d.). AZQuotes.com. Retrieved February 17, 2020, from AZQuotes.com Web site: https://www.azquotes.com/author/4399-Albert_Einstein.

Einstein, Albert. Quotes. (n.d.). BrainyQuote.com. Retrieved February 18, 2020, from BrainyQuote.com Web site: https://www.brainyquote.com/quotes/albert_einstein_145949

Ekvall, G. (1983). Climate, structure and innovativeness of organizations: A theoretical framework and an experiment. Stockholm, Sweden: The Swedish Council for Management and Organizational Behaviour.

Evans, B. (1993). Everyday Wonders. Contemporary Books. Chicago, IL.

Evans, J., Frankish, K. (2009). In Two Minds: Dual Processes and Beyond. New York: Oxford University Press.

Fingeroth, D. (2004). Superman on the Couch. New York, NY: The Continuum International Publishing Group Inc.

Firestien, R. L. (1996). Leading on the creative edge: Gaining competitive advantage through the power of Creative Problem Solving. Colorado Springs, CO: Pinon Press.

Frankl, V. (1984). Man's Search for Meaning: An Introduction to Logotherapy. 3rd ed. New York: Simon & Shuster.

Friedman, R.S., Forster, J. (2005). Effects of motivational cues on perceptual asymmetry: implications for creativity and analytical problem solving. Journal of Personality and Social Psychology; Feb; 88 (2): 263-275.

Fritz, R. (1994). The path of least resistance: Learning to become the creative force in your own life. New York: Fawcett-Columbine.

Fry, W. (1994). The biology of humor. Humor: International Journal of Humor Research, 7, 111-126.

Gardner, H. (1983). Frames of mind: The theory of multiple intelligences. New York, NY: Basic Books.

Gerber, T. Becoming Jane Goodall. National Geographic October 2017 Vol. 232, No. 4.

Gertner, J. (2012). The Idea Factory. New York, NY: Penguin Group.

Goleman, D., Kaufman, P., Ray, M. (1993). The Creative Spirit. New York, NY: Penguin Group.

Gordon, W. J. J. (1961). Synectics, NYC: Harper & Row.

Guilford, J. P. (1967). The Nature of Human Intelligence. NYC: McGraw Hill.

Halberstam, D. (1989). Summer of 49. William Morrow Paperbacks.

Hecht, D. (2013). The Neural Basis of Optimism and Pessimism. Experimental Neurobiology v22(3); PMC 3807005.

Herrmann, N. (1989). The Creative Brain. Lake Lure, NC: Brain Books.

Icekson, T., Roskes, M., Moran, S. (2014) Effects of optimism on creativity under approach and avoidance motivation. Frontiers in Human Neuroscience v8; PMC 3937876.

Isaacson, W. (2007). Einstein: His Life and Universe. New York: Simon & Schuster.

Isaksen, S. G. (1983). Toward a model for the facilitation of creative problem solving. The Journal of Creative Behavior, 17 (1), 18-31.

Isaksen, S. G., Dorval, K. B., & Treffinger, D. J. (2000). Creative approaches to problem solving 2nd ed.). Dubuque, IA: Kendall/Hunt Publishing.

Isaksen, S. G. & Treffinger, D.J. (1985). Creative problem solving: the basic course. Buffalo, NY: Bearly Limited.

Jane Goodall Institute Website (2017). Vienna, VA.

Janis, I (1982). Groupthink, Second Edition. Wadsworth Cengage Learning.

Johnson, S. (2010). Where Good Ideas Come From. New York, NY: Riverhead Books.

Jung, R., Wertz, C., Meadows, C., Ryman, S., Vakhtin, A., Flores, R. (2015). Quantity yields quality when it comes to creativity: a brain and behavioral test of the equal-odds rule. Frontiers in Psychology, V6.

Kanji, G. K. & Asher, M. (1996). 100 methods for Total Quality Management. London: Sage.

Kaufman, S. (2013). The Real Neuroscience of Creativity. Scientific American Blog Network.

Kaufman, S. (2018). My Quest to Understand Human Intelligence. To appear in R. J. Sternberg. The Nature of Human Intelligence. Cambridge University Press.

Keller-Mathers, S., and Murdock, M. (2008). A Teaching Model for Integrating Creativity into Content. International Center for Studies in Creativity at Buffalo State, Buffalo, NY.

Kirton, M. J. (1976). Adaptors and innovators: A description and measure. Journal of Applied Psychology, 61, 622-629.

Kriegel, R., Patler, L. (1991). If it ain't broke... Break it.

Leff, H. (1984). Playful Perception. Waterfront Books and Herbert Leff.

Leonard, K. & Yorton, T. (2015). Yes, And. *New York*: Harper Collins.

Limb, C., Barret, K., Barret, F., Jiradeivong, P., Rankin, S., & Landau, A. (2020). Classical Creativity. A functional MRI investigation of pianist and improviser Gabriela Montero. Neuroimage. Apr 1: 209: 116496, Epub 2019 Dec 30,

Lewis Carroll Quotes. (n.d.). BrainyQuote. com. Retrieved February 16, 2020, from BrainyQuote.com Web site: https://www.brainyquote.com/quotes/lewis_carroll_165865.

McGinnis, A. L. (1985). Bringing out the best in people. *Minneapolis, MN*: Augsburg Publishing House.

Medina, J. (2014). Your Best Brain. The Great Courses. Chantilly, VA.

Michalko, M. (1991). Thinkertoys. Berkeley, CA: Ten Speed.

Miller, B., Vehar J. & Firestien R. (2001). Creativity unbound (3rd ed.).

Morris, E. (2010). Colonel Roosevelt. New York: Random House.

Noller, R. B., Parnes, S. J., & Biondi, A.M. (1976). Creative actionbook. NYC: Charles Scribner's Sons.

Oliver Wendell Holmes, Sr. Quotes. (n.d.). BrainyQuote.com. Retrieved February 17, 2020, from BrainyQuote.com Web site: https://www.brainyquote.com/quotes/oliver_wendell_holmes_sr_104426

Oppezzo, M. & Schwartz, D. (2014). Give your ideas some legs: The positive effects of walking on creative thinking.

Journal of Experimental Psychology: Learning, Memory, and Cognition, 40(4), 1142 – 1152.

Osborn, A. F. (1993). Applied imagination: Principles and procedures of Creative Problem-Solving (3rd ed.) *Buffalo, NY*: The Creative Education Foundation Press.

Paige, S. (2014). The Very Best of Winston Churchill. Amazon Digital Services.

Parnes, S. J. (1967). Creative behavior guidebook. *New York*: Scribner.

Parnes, S. J. (1981). The magic of your mind. *Buffalo, NY*: The Creative Education Foundation.

Parnes, S. J. (1992). Source Book for Creative Thinking: *Buffalo, NY*: Creative Education Foundation.

Parnes, S. J. (1988). Visioning. *Buffalo, NY*: Creative Education Foundation.

Pasteur, L. (2016). Famous Scientists, famousscientists.org.

Pollack, J. (2014). Shortcut. *New York*: Gotham Books.

Pressfield, S. (2012). The War of Art. *New York*,: Black Irish Entertainment.

Prince, G. M. (1973). The practice of creativity: NYC: Collier.

Provine, R. (2001). Laughter: A Scientific Investigation. Penguin Books. New York, NY.

Puccio, G. J., Murdock, M. C., & Mance. M. (2005). Current developments in creative problem solving for organizations: A focus on thinking skills and styles. The Korean Journal of Thinking & Problem Solving, 15(2). 43076.

Puccio, G. J. (2013). The Creative Thinkers Toolkit (audio book). The Great Courses. Chantilly, VA.

William Watson Purkey.AZ Quotes.com. Retrieved February 17, 2020, from AZQuotes.com Web site: https://www. azquotes.com/quote/880130

Ramos H. (2017). Cognitive Fixation and Creativity. In: Carayannis E. (eds) Encyclopedia of Creativity, Invention, Innovation and Entrepreneurship. Springer, New York, NY

Ratey, J. (2013). Spark. New York, NY: Little, Brown and Company.

Ray, M. and Myers, R. (1986). Creativity in Business. Garden City, NY: Doubleday.

Rosenman, S. (1933). Franklin D. Roosevelt Inaugural Address March 4, 1933. The Public Papers of Franklin D. Roosevelt, Volume Two: The Year of Crisis, 1933 (New York: Random House, 1938), 11–16.

Schultz, C. (2013). Schackleton Probably Never Took Out an ad Seeking Men for a Hazardous Journey. Smithsonian.com.

Sims, P. (2011). Little Bets. New York, NY: Simon and Schuster.

Senge, P. M., Kleiner, A., Roberts, C., Ross, R. B., & Smith, B. J. (1994). The Fifth Discipline Fieldbook. New York: Doubleday.

Sharot, T. (2011). The optimism bias. Current Biology. Volume 21, Issue 23, pR941-R945.

Shekerjian, D. (1990). Uncommon genius. New York, NY: Viking Penguin.

Simonton, D. K. (1981). Creativity in Western civilization; Extrinsic and intrinsic causes. American Anthropologist, 83, 628-630.

Simonton, D. (1997). Creative Productivity: a predictive and explanatory model of career trajectories and landmarks. Psychol. Rev. 104, 66-89.

Sood, A. (2013). The Mayo Clinic Guide to Stress-Free Living. De Capo Press.

Srivasta, S. & Copperrider, D. L. (1999). Appreciative management and leadership. The power of positive thought and action in Organization. Euclid, OH: Williams Custom Publishing.

Sternberg, R. J. (1999). Handbook of creativity. Cambridge University Press.

Sternberg, R. J., & Lubart, T. I. (1991). An investment theory of creativity and its development. Human Development, 34(1), 1-31.

Sutton, R. (2002). Weird Ideas that Work. New York, NY: The Free Press.

Tharp, T. (2003). The Creative Habit. New York, NY: Simon & Schuster

Torrance, E. P. (1972). Can we teach children to think creatively? The Journal of Creative Behavior, 6, 114-143.

Torrance, E. and Safter, T. (1999). Making the creative leap beyond. The Creative Education Foundation Press.

Treffinger, D. J. (1996). Dimensions of creativity. Idea Capsule # 9004. Sarasota, FL: Center for Creative Learning.

U.S. Department of Health and Human Services Physical Activity Guidelines for Americans, 2nd edition (2018).

Washington, DC: US Department of Health and Human Services.

VanGundy, A. B. (1988). Techniques of structured problem solving. New York: Van Nostrand Reinhold.

VanGundy, A. B. (1992). Idea power: Techniques and resources to unleash the creativity in your organization. New York: AMACOM.

Von Oech, R. (1998). A whack on the side of the head (3rd ed.). New York: Warner Books.

Wieman, H. N. (1958). Man's ultimate commitment. Southern Illinois University Press.

Wigert, B., Robinson, J. (2018). Fostering Creativity at Work: Do your Mangers Push or Crush Innovation. Gallup Workplace.

Wilson, L. and Wilson, H. (1998). Play to Win. Choosing Growth over Fear in Work and Life. Austin, TX. Bard Press, Inc.

Wright, T. (June, 2007). How Things Work: Electromagnetic Catapults. Air & Space Magazine

Zaccaro, S. (2001). The Nature of Organizational Leadership. San Francisco, CA: Jossey-Bass Inc.

INDEX

C

E

F

J

N

Q

R

S